The Saint's Treasury

Jeremiah Burroughs

Monergism Books

Contents

To the Honourable, Francis Rous,

E sq Speaker of the Parliament of the Commonwealth of England, and Provost of Eaton College. Honoured Sir,

IF a Heathen Poet could say, "Non omnis moriar," I shall live though I die; assuming his Works immortal, though he himself were mortal; Upon how much better an account may a Prophet of the Lord say, "Non moriar, sed vivam," I shall not die, but live; both in respect of his immortal soul, to which death is as the gate of life; and in respect of the immortal travail of his soul, being conversant in the Word of the Lord that abides forever.

The works of the Saints of God in whom is the spirit of prophecy not only live when they are dead, but are instrumental in the hand of grace, both to plant life where it is not, and water it where it is, that it may spring forth more abundantly.

The chosen Vessel of the Lord, by whose Ministry he was pleased to give out the Heavenly treasures laid up in these Sermons, has some years since put off his earthly, and put on that Inheritance of the Saints in light, for which the Lord seemed early to have fitted him, by his earnest and assiduous Travail in assisting others. But though the Vessel be broken, or rather indeed refined and translated to his master's more immediate use, yet the Treasures abide for the common enrichment of the Saints. For spiritual Treasures (like the loaves blessed by our Saviour) multiply in their use, and when thousands have been enriched by them, do still remain sufficient to enrich thousands.

To you, honoured Sir, is this small but precious treasury presented, not as though your own store were not already full; for who knows not how many precious jewels (through the riches of Christ in you) you have richly set and polished for adorning the Bride, the Lamb's wife? Surely the spirit of Christ seems to have chosen and sealed your Spirit to celebrate his own Nuptials in your Mystical Marriage and song of loves.

But as gold, besides its own internal worth, receives an authentic impression from the Image and Superscription of the Prince: And as in honouring the Lord with the best part of our substance, An humble acknowledgment of his Interest both in the whole and ourselves (not any Addition to his fullness) is intended: So is this Treasury presented to the touch and test of your Judgment, First as the Standard of approving things that are excellent. And then as an humble testimony how much he owes himself to you who presents it.

That the Lord would make you long an Ornament and defense to his Saints, and prosper his own pleasure in your hands, is the prayer of,

Honoured Sir,

The most humble, and most obliged of your Servants, J. W.

To the Christian Reader.

The Author of these ensuing Sermons has so abundantly proved himself to the Church of God through his previous labours, both in preaching and writing, that it would be rather a disservice to him to offer anything by way of commendation. His name is still like precious ointment, and may it remain so as long as the Sun and Moon endure. These Sermons will reveal themselves to be his authentic work; the various characteristics and qualities of his style (though styles differ as much as faces) are discernible here. Those who had the privilege of being in his company and hearing him can attest, "Sic oculos, sic ill manus, sic ora ferebat" - thus he explained his Text, thus he handled his Doctrine, thus he delivered his Application. It is true, these remnants of his are under the prejudice of being posthumous works; yet we may say of them as Paul said concerning himself, "We suppose they are not inferior to the rest of his Works, though they are born out of due time," and though they are fragments, they are still to be esteemed as "Ramenta auri sunt pretiosa." These Sermons are valuable in their own right and intrinsic excellence, regardless of the author. And this Author is to be honoured for his true worth, whatever else he may have authored.

We shall also add this for your encouragement: these Sermons have been faithfully transcribed by the hand of a skilled writer, Mr. Farthing, who is now a Teacher of Shorthand, and who has demonstrated his exceptional skill and dexterity in shorthand writing. We believe we can confidently say that there are very few words spoken by the Author that have been omitted. Moreover, we are confident that nothing of significance from his preaching has been omitted; it has all been faithfully presented to you through the diligence of the Scribe.

The publishers' desire is that the name of this worthy man of God may be held in honour, that you may apply these teachings to your own life, and that what was spoken to some may become common to all; what was accepted by those who heard it may be received and improved upon by those who read it. This is all we have to convey to you; it would be unjust to detain you any longer from the esteemed Author. We only commend you to the grace of God, which is capable of enabling you to excel in every good work, and bid you Farewell.

Ja. Nalton. Will. Cooper. Tho. Jacomb. Matthew Poole. Allen Geare. Ralph Venning: September. 29. 1653.

Imprimatur,

EDM. CALAMY.

The Incomparable Excellence and Holiness of God.

Who is like unto you, O Lord, among the gods! Who
is like you, glorious in holiness, awe-inspiring in praises,
performing wonders! – Exodus 15. 11.

T his Scripture is today fulfilled in our ears and before our eyes;
what God has already begun to do for this Kingdom and the
neighbouring Churches shows us that there is none like the Lord, who
is glorious in holiness, awe-inspiring in praises, performing wonders.

Though these words are in the middle of the song, they serve as a
kind of epiphonema, which is usually at the end. However, Moses, in
his admiration and praise of God for the great things He had done for
His people, cannot contain himself until the end and bursts forth in
the middle with this applause of the glory of God: "Who is like unto
you, O Lord among the gods! Who is like you, glorious in holiness,

awe-inspiring in praises, performing wonders!" These words are a part
of Moses's song, occasioned by God's goodness in delivering His people
from Egypt and leading them through the Red Sea. This song is the most
ancient song in the world, the first in Scripture, and there is no known
author before Moses. Those skilled in poetry came many centuries after
Moses. It is a spiritual and excellent song, full of elegance in style and rich
in variety of content. It is Eucharistic, triumphant, and prophetic, and
it's a pity that we don't have such an excellent song as this one set to meter
to be sung in our congregations. It's also a delightful song, and you'll
observe that when God promised a great mercy to His people, causing
them to rejoice greatly, He referred to this song (Hosea 2:15). When
God intended a significant blessing for His people, He wanted them
to sing a song like Moses's. Therefore, if God is showing us His mercy
and opening a door of hope, this song is timely. It's a typological song,
representing the deliverance of God's people from Egypt and serving as a
type of their liberation from the bondage of Antichrist. It's significant to
note that this song will be sung again when God's people are delivered
from Antichrist. In Revelation 15, you can see God's judgments upon
Antichrist, and in verse 3, it is said that they sing the song of Moses,
the servant of God, and the song of the Lamb, saying, "Great and mar-
velous are your works, Lord God Almighty; just and true are your ways,
you King of Saints." This shows us that God wants to convey that the
bondage under Antichrist is akin to the bondage in Egypt, and that's why
Rome is referred to as Egypt in the Book of Revelation because when
we are delivered from Antichristian bondage, we will renew this song of
Moses. Therefore, if we are anticipating deliverance from the bondage
under Antichrist, it is wise for us to acquaint ourselves with this song,
as it will be sung again when the bondage of Antichrist is removed. This
song is considered miraculous according to the opinion of Augustine.
He presents this song as one of the miracles, suggesting that at the same
time, God inspired all the people of Israel by the Spirit to sing the same

song together. While this would be truly miraculous, the Scripture is not clear on this matter.

But we leave generals and come to the words; though there are many excellent things in the Chapter to prepare the way for what I have read, I will go straight to the words without delay. These words are, in a way, a summary of everything, containing the essence of it all. It's as if he said, "I have spoken about many specific things that God does for His people, but there is no one like the Lord, who is glorious in holiness, awe-inspiring in praises, performing wonders." So, there are four aspects (you can see) in which God's name is exalted here: Firstly, there is no one like the Lord. Secondly, glorious in holiness. Thirdly, awe-inspiring in praises. Fourthly, performing wonders.

I must admit that when I first considered speaking on this Text, I intended to focus only on the third aspect, the explanation of that Title of God, "awe-inspiring in praises." I can't find any similar title in the entire book of God except in this place. However, since I realized there is a lot of significance in the first two aspects related to God, I thought it might be helpful to show you what they reveal about God and was reluctant to skip them. So, regarding the first two, "Who is like you, O Lord, among the gods, who is like you, glorious in holiness, who is like you?" You can see that this is posed as a question, and in Scripture, questions serve two main purposes: First, by way of admiration. Second, by way of negation. Sometimes, by way of admiration, as in Isaiah 63:1, "Who is this that comes from Edom with dyed garments from Bozrah!" There are many other examples of admiration. By way of negation, you know there are hundreds of examples. Both of these meanings apply here in the Text. First, by way of admiration, "Who is like unto you, O Lord, among the gods, etc." Moses and the people, struck with astonishment at the glory of God now manifested through His great works, admire and say, "Who is like unto you, O Lord?" Then, by way of negation, "Who is like unto you, O Lord?" That is, there is no one like you. This is the first expression of the glory of God, exalting the name of God above all things; there is no one like God.

God takes great glory in this expression of His glory, that there is no one like Him. We find it frequently in Scripture, as in 1 Chronicles 17:20, "O Lord, there is none like you, neither is there any God besides you, according to all that we have heard with our ears." Similarly, in Psalm 86:8, "Among the gods, there is none like unto you, O Lord." And in Psalm 89:6, "For who in the heaven can be compared unto the Lord? Who among the sons of the mighty can be likened unto the Lord?" There are many other places where God takes pride in this expression of His glory, and the people of God have also celebrated it. There is good reason for them to do so. It is said of the godly Maccabees that, at first, their name was offensive to some. However, upon encountering this sentence, "Who is like unto you, O Lord, among the gods?" and being deeply impressed by it, they inscribed the first Hebrew letter of every word in this sentence on their war banners and carried them with them. On this basis, they were called the Maccabees, boasting in this Title of God, "Who is like unto you?" The Holy Ghost, on this ground, concludes that all should honour and glorify God because there is no one like Him. In Psalm 86:8, it says, "Among the gods, there is none like unto you, O Lord; neither are there any works like unto your works." Take note of what follows in verses 9-12. "All Nations whom you have made shall come and worship before you, O Lord, and shall glorify your name; for you are great and do wondrous things; for you are God alone. Teach me your way, O Lord; I will walk in your truth; unite my heart to fear your name; I will praise you, O Lord, my God, with all my heart, and I will glorify your Name forevermore." You can see how the holy Prophet was captivated by this expression of God, that there is no one like Him. Therefore, "teach me your way, O Lord; I will walk in your truth," etc.

There is none like unto the Lord among the gods. So, it may be translated just as well among the mighties. God is elevated here not only above the heathen gods, so that there is none like Him among them, but He is exalted above anything that possesses excellence in it. There is none like you among the mighties, no matter how mighty and great, no matter what greatness and excellence there may be in the world, God is infinitely superior to all. It would consume too much time if we were to extensively discuss the glory of God in this regard—how He is above all things, and that there is none like Him. Therefore, I will briefly mention a few points, apply this particular, and move on to the second, which we will dwell on for a longer time.

There is none like God: First, in that everything that is in God is God Himself. This is a unique characteristic of God; no creature possesses such excellence, where everything in it constitutes its being. All creatures are composed of various elements, but in God, whatever is in Him is God Himself. Furthermore, there is universal goodness in God, and there is none like Him in that regard. One creature has one good quality, and another has another. But God possesses all goodness within Him; all excellence and beauty exist in God in an eminent manner. There is none like Him in this regard. Moreover, all attributes in God are but one excellence. Though we may perceive God through various attributes, and one attribute may shine through one creature while another shines through another, they are all united in God. Everything in Him is intrinsically in Him; He is self-existent, self-originating, and self-oriented. No one can communicate themselves in the way God can. No one can inflict evil or convey good in the manner God can, and this expression of God has reference to that fact. It is unique to God to bestow as much of Himself as He pleases, which no creature can do. Although a creature possesses only a small amount of goodness compared to the infinite abundance in God, it cannot communicate even those small drops of goodness as it wishes; it is God's exclusive prerogative to impart His goodness as He wills. Not only that, but He can make the creature to whom He conveys His goodness as aware of that goodness as He desires, which no one else can achieve. Even if one creature communicates good to another, it cannot make the recipient as aware of that good as it wishes, but God can do so. In inflicting evil, there is none like the Lord in that respect; the Lord is capable of releasing all evil, of bringing all evil at once, something no one else can do. He can also make the creature upon whom He inflicts evil as aware of that evil as He pleases. One who harms another cannot make the victim as aware of that harm as they desire, but this is God's unique prerogative. Just as He can unleash all evil at once, He is able to make the creature as conscious of all of it as He wills. God claims this as His exclusive prerogative, that only He can do good and only He can do evil. Therefore, there is none like Him. From this, it follows that there is no one to be worshipped as the Lord, no one to be honoured as the Lord. The heathen gods, because they only conveyed some specific good, therefore demanded only particular service—external worship and worship in some specifics were sufficient for the heathen gods, and they were content with it and required nothing more. This was reasonable because they could not claim a universal good for themselves. One god represented one particular good, and another represented another particular good. Therefore, they received specific worship corresponding to their domain. However, there is none like the Lord. He demands universal worship and obedience. "You shall worship the Lord your God with all your heart, soul, and strength." No other being is to be worshipped in the same way as God. All of this is because there is none like Him in the excellence of His nature and in the manner of communicating Himself to His creatures.

Now, what I have said is exceedingly useful in the entire course of our lives, in directing our thoughts and actions toward God. Consider how beneficial this is in the following way: It should be our concern, when we perceive any beauty, goodness, or excellence in a creature, to always maintain in our thoughts and hearts the awareness of the infinite distance between God and that creature. The absence of this awareness is the root cause of nearly all the evil in the world, and the genuine understanding of this fact is a special means to empower us to glorify God as God. I mean this: when you observe any excellence, beauty, or attractiveness in a creature and taste any sweetness in it, be certain that you retain in your heart the awareness of this truth—although there may be some sweetness here, God is infinitely superior to the creature, and there is an infinite disproportion between the goodness, beauty, and excellence in these creatures and that which is in God Himself. God allows us to pour out our hearts upon and derive comfort from the creature when we see beauty and excellence in it. This is because it bears His likeness and contains His excellence. A spiritual heart has greater freedom to open itself to the comforts of the creature than anyone else in the world because it can encounter and experience God there. However, even though God permits us to do this, we must always ensure that our hearts remain reserved for God and that we remain aware of the infinite excellence present in God above any creature. If we are not careful about this, we will quickly deviate from glorifying God as God, and our hearts will become attached to the creature. This has been the basis for all outward and spiritual idolatry in the world. In the case of outward idolatry, it arose like this: initially, people recognised that the Sun, Moon, and Stars were creatures and that there was more excellence in God than in any of these celestial objects. However, as they began to focus too much on the creature and became captivated by the excellence they saw there, their hearts became attached to the creature. They lost the awareness of the infinite excellence of God above the creature and subsequently turned away from God to worship those that were not gods.

The same holds true for spiritual idolatry. Those who commit idolatry with riches or any other creature first acknowledge that there is infinitely more in God than in the creature. However, by lavishing their hearts on the creature and fixating on its beauty, they eventually lose the initial awareness that was in their hearts and commit spiritual idolatry with the creature. Therefore, we must take care to preserve our awareness and sense of the infinite distance between God and all the comforts of the creature. As long as you maintain your fresh and strong awareness in this regard, there is no danger, and you do not sin by indulging in the creature. If it has not diminished your awareness of the infinite disproportion between God and all creatures, there is no issue. Now, since there is an infinitely staggering level of excellence in God above all creatures, our thoughts towards God and the creature should be similar. Just as there is an infinite distance between the excellence of God and the excellence of all creatures, there should be a sort of infinity in the gap and disproportion between the esteem, joy, and reliance we have in and upon the creature compared to what we have in and upon God. Therefore, you should not be content with merely acknowledging that God surpasses the creature, for everyone does so. Instead, you should find in your souls such an imbalance between your estimation, delight, and dependence on the creature versus what you have for God, somewhat resembling the infinite gap between God and the creature. The distance is indeed infinite between God and the creature; therefore, there should be a kind of infiniteness in the distance between your regard for, your enthusiasm in pursuing, and your efforts towards the creature and what you exhibit toward God. This is how you glorify God as God; this is the soulful worship we owe to God in the world. This is the true sanctification of the name of God when it becomes practical in our hearts.

Secondly, if there is none like God, then it logically follows that there is no one like the people of God. As a person's god is, so is the person. Look at it this way: Whichever god a person chooses, they become like their god. For instance, a covetous person, if they make riches their god, should be judged accordingly. The same applies to a voluptuous person or a heathen. Now, if the saints of God have chosen this God to be their God, and there is no one like Him, it must necessarily follow that there is no people like God's people. Notice how the Holy Spirit draws this connection in various Scriptures, such as Deuteronomy 33:26 and 33:29. In verse 26, it says, "There is none like unto the God of Jeshurun, who rideth upon the heaven in thy help and in his excellency in the sky." What is the conclusion the Holy Spirit makes here? In verse 29, it says, "Happy art thou, O Israel: who is like unto thee, O people saved by the Lord," and so on. Therefore, according to the glory of God in any particular, there is a reflection of it upon the saints of God. This is the wonderful excellence of God's saints—to have the reflection of God upon them. Happy are those who have God as their God; if God is excellent, so are they. If God is above all, and there is no one like Him, then they are above all, and there is no one like them. The same inference can be found in 2 Samuel 7:22-23, where it says, "Wherefore thou art great, O Lord God, for there is none like thee, neither is there any God besides thee; according to all that we have heard with our ears. And what one nation in the earth is like thy people, even like Israel?" Therefore, there is no one like the people of God. It logically follows that they are as their God is. Thus, when Moses speaks of the people of God in Exodus 33:16, he says, "So shall we be separated, I and thy people, from all the people that are upon the earth." However, the original Hebrew word signifies "wonderfully separated." God's people are wonderfully separated from the world, just as God is wonderfully high above all creatures. Therefore, in Numbers 23:9, it is said that God's people shall dwell alone and shall not be reckoned among the nations because they are the people of God and the people of that God who has no equal. Thus, there is no one like them, and this is a source of comfort for the saints of God.

Thirdly, it follows from this that we should take care to ensure that no one does more for their gods than we do for ours. If there is no one like our God, then it is a shame that those who choose other gods should do more for them than we do for our God. This applies to both outward and spiritual idolatry. For instance, consider idolaters: none of them have a God as great as ours. Their rock is not as our rock, and even their enemies acknowledge this. How shameful would it be if we did not do more for our God than they do for theirs? Indeed, we should strive to do for our God what matches the excellence that we perceive in Him. Let's examine what idolaters do for their gods. Firstly, observe the earnestness of idolaters' hearts when it comes to their gods. Their hearts are inflamed with passion for their idols. This can be seen in Isaiah 57:5, which says, "Enflaming yourselves with idols under every green tree." Their hearts are enflamed with their idol gods, which are not like our God. So, how much more should our hearts be enflamed for our God? Should we be content with lukewarm and lifeless service to our God? This is why the exhortation of the Apostle in Romans 12:11 should have a strong impact on us: "Be fervent in spirit, serving the Lord." We are serving the Lord, our God, the great and glorious God, and therefore, we should be fervent in spirit in His service.

Secondly, the Scripture says that idolaters, those who worship false gods, are mad about their idols. In Jeremiah 50:38, it is stated, "The people of God, therefore, should have their hearts set on God in such a way that those who are carnal and unable to discern properly would consider them as madmen. In fact, that is how they are often viewed: when the hearts of the saints are fully focused on God, they are perceived as madmen. For instance, the Apostle Paul was considered a madman by Festus, as mentioned in Acts 26:24. We should not be afraid of the world's reproaches in this regard. Even though they despise us, regard us as base and foolish, and think we are out of our minds, we should not be deterred. After all, idolaters are mad about their idols. Therefore, if God demands something from us, even if the world considers it madness, our hearts must pursue God in it. It would be a shame for anyone's heart to be more devoted to their gods than ours because there is no one like our God.

Thirdly, the intensity of idolaters' hearts towards their idol gods is evident from Jeremiah 8:1-2. It says, "At that time, saith the Lord, they shall bring out the bones of the Kings of Judah, etc. And they shall spread them before the Sun, and the Moon, and all the host of Heaven, whom they have loved, and whom they have served, and after whom they have walked, and whom they have sought, and whom they have worshipped; they shall not be gathered, nor be buried," and so on. I have often pondered this Scripture; it is remarkably expressive. I cannot think of any Scripture in the entire Bible that contains so many expressions together to illustrate the fervor of God's people's hearts towards God as we find here to demonstrate the zeal of idolaters towards their idols: "And they shall spread them before the Sun, and the Moon, and all the host of Heaven." Notice the five aspects mentioned: 1. Whom they have loved. 2. Whom they have served. 3. After whom they have walked. 4. Whom they have sought. 5. Whom they have worshipped. All of this is conveyed in just a few words. Their hearts were wholly devoted to their idol gods. How much more, then, should it be said of us concerning our God, whom we have loved, served, walked after, sought, and worshipped?

Furthermore, consider how the Scripture portrays the devotion of people to their idol gods in terms of the cost they are willing to incur. In Isaiah 46:6, it states, "They shall lavish gold out of the bag, and weigh silver in the balance, and hire a goldsmith, and he maketh it a god." They spare no expense to worship their idols. What a shame it would be if we were not willing to part with a significant portion of our wealth for the true worship of the true God. Even if we were to lose our possessions, we should be content if we can serve God better and in a purer way. Idolaters will spare no expense for their idols. Now, there is none like our God; therefore, it is a disgrace that they should do more for their gods than we do for ours. Additionally, consider what idolaters are willing to endure for their gods. In 1 Kings 18:28, we see how Baal's priests cut themselves with knives and lances until blood gushed out to show their devotion to their idols. Let us, therefore, be willing to endure anything that God calls us to endure. How faithful were idolaters to their idols!

This is why God says in Jeremiah 2:10-11, "Consider diligently and see if there be such a thing: hath a nation changed their gods which are yet no gods? but my people have changed their glory for that which doth not profit." God takes great offense that idolaters do not change their gods, who are infinitely below Him, while His people change their God, who is infinitely above them.

Furthermore, let us be cautious lest there are those who set their hearts more on their lusts than we do on God. Take all the excellencies in the world, and they are infinitely inferior to God; how much more, then, is a lust? For what is a lust compared to all creatures in heaven and earth? Yet, how passionately do men's hearts desire their lusts? How has your own heart been consumed by wicked desires in the past? Consider, then, how infinitely unreasonable it is for any person's heart in the world, or your own heart, to be more captivated by a base lust than by the living, eternal, and infinite God. It is said of Ahab that he sold himself to work wickedness (1 Kings 21:20). Therefore, be willing to sell yourself to God, to surrender yourself to God. It is said that the hearts of the sons of men are set, and fully set to do evil (Ecclesiastes 8:11). Do not content yourself with mere wishes and desires for God; instead, let your heart be fully devoted to God. In Micah 7:3, it is stated that they do evil with both hands earnestly. Note that they do evil, and they do it earnestly, and they do it earnestly with both hands. Therefore, do not be sluggish in serving your God; do what is good, do it with both your hands, and do it earnestly with all your heart.

Again, we have one notable Scripture that demonstrates how the hearts of men are inclined towards evil, Proverbs 19:28. "The mouth of the wicked devours iniquity" is an elegant expression from the Holy Ghost. It's a metaphor drawn from the behavior of animals. Just as if you take a beast that has been deprived of water for a long time and is exceedingly thirsty, when you bring it to the water, it will thrust its head into the water as if it would consume the entire river and could never be satisfied. That's the meaning of the phrase "the mouth of the wicked devours iniquity." It means that when a wicked person engages in sin, they are as eager for it as a thirsty beast is for water Oh, how much more should our hearts be infinitely more eager for God and His service than wicked people are or can be for the service of their lusts! To conclude this point, consider Exodus 30, from verse 34 to the end. There, a perfume was to be made according to the composition of the Apothecary, but there was this charge given: "As for the perfume which thou shalt make, you shall not make to yourselves, according to the composition thereof, it shall be unto thee holy for the Lord," and so on. Thus, I conclude this point: there is none like God, as He is above all. Therefore, when your hearts are in any good disposition towards God, perfumed and lifted up towards God, beware that they are not lifted up towards any creature in the same manner as they are towards God. Your service to God must be in accordance with the nature of God. Since there is none like God, no one should receive the same level of service as God. This concludes the first aspect of God's name being exalted here: "Who is like unto thee, O Lord, among the gods!"

Now we move on to the second aspect: "glorious in holiness." The word translated here as "glorious" can also mean magnificent and noble, and it is used in many places in that sense. "Thou art magnificent and noble in thy holiness." Brethren, the greatest magnificence, the highest nobility, and the loftiest spirit that can exist is to be holy. God Himself is a magnificent God, and He is ennobled by His holiness. This demonstrates the excellence of holiness.

Furthermore, "glorious in holiness" can also be understood as "glorious in holy things," signifying that God is glorious in His holy Angels, holy Saints, holy word, holy Ordinances, and holy worship. God is indeed very glorious in His Angels, Saints, word, worship, and Ordinances, but for the purpose of this discussion, we will take the words as they are presented here: "glorious in holiness."

To explain the glory of God in this Title, there are three things to address: First, I will briefly explain what holiness in God is. Second, I will elucidate how God is described as glorious in holiness. Third, I will explain why God is given this Title here in this passage, why He is described as glorious in holiness rather than glorious in power, even though His act of power was evident in the destruction of the Egyptians and the deliverance of His people.

For the first aspect: what is holiness in God? We generally understand this, as we do almost all things of God, more by way of negation than otherwise—more by what it is not than by what it is. Therefore, we commonly say that God's holiness is that quality by which His nature is free from all kinds of mixture and the slightest stain or filth of sin. Hence, God is called light because light is such a pure creature and free from any mixture of impurity that it can be among filthy things without becoming defiled. In the same way, God can work with sin itself without any defilement of His nature. But besides this negation, if you want to know something positive about God's holiness, I would describe it briefly like this: It is the infinite uprightness and perfection of God's will, especially His will, by which He wills and accomplishes all things in harmony with the infinite excellence of His own being. God's excellence is the highest and, therefore, the standard for all excellence. Since God's will is always in harmony with His infinite excellence and cannot deviate in the least from it, His will becomes the standard for all holiness. Let's understand this a bit better by looking at the holiness of creatures, and through that, we can gain some insight into the holiness of God. Just as we cannot directly look at the sun's glory because it is too bright for our eyes, we can behold its radiance by observing its reflection in water. Similarly, God's holiness is too bright to be seen directly. We cannot behold the infinite purity and holiness of God firsthand. However, by observing the holiness of creatures, which is like a reflection of God's holiness upon them, a ray and beam of it, we can gain some understanding of God's holiness. Now, the holiness of a creature is essentially the separation of that creature from common things for a holy purpose or the consecration of a creature in a special way to God for the exaltation of God's name. The holiness of the Saints consists of the separation of their spirits from all common things to God as the highest and ultimate end. When they can work for God as the ultimate end and will what they do in relation to God as the final end, and in a manner that is appropriate for God as the highest end, that is the holiness of their wills. The same principle applies to God's holiness. God's holiness is like a dedication of God to Himself. God, being of Himself and from Himself, with Himself as His last end, gives Himself up to Himself and wills Himself as the highest and ultimate end. Consequently, He wills all things in relation to Himself as the last and highest end. This is the holiness of God, and the image of this holiness is the mark and work of grace upon the creature. When the creature is empowered to will God as the highest end and all things in subordination to Him, the creature is then said to be holy because it bears the imprint of God. This is God's holiness.

But "glorious in holiness"—how is God glorious in holiness? God is glorious in all His attributes and works. The truth is that there is not one thing in God that is more glorious than another. Every attribute of God is equally glorious in itself. However, in terms of manifestation and our perception, one aspect may appear more glorious than another. God speaks to us according to our understanding. Therefore, you can see how the Saints especially glorify God as a holy God. They rejoice greatly and glorify Him when they consider Him as holy. This is why the Psalmist says in Psalm 99:3, "Let them praise thy great and terrible name, for it is holy." And in verse 5, "Exalt ye the Lord our God, and worship at his footstool, for he is holy." And again in verse 9, "Exalt the Lord our God and worship at his holy hill, for the Lord our God is holy." The people of God view God's holiness as the special basis for His praise and exaltation. Even the Angels in heaven regard God in His holiness and exalt Him, as seen in Isaiah 6:3, where the Cherubim and Seraphim cry out three times, "Holy, holy, holy is the Lord of hosts." You won't find any of God's attributes mentioned three times in a row like this. Although it is true that God is infinite in power and wisdom, you will not find in Scripture that God is described as wise, wise, wise or almighty, almighty, almighty. However, the word "holy" is repeated three times. As the Angels in Heaven adore God especially for His holiness, so does the Church of God, as seen in Revelation 4:8. They cry out, "Holy, holy, holy, Lord God almighty," demonstrating the blessed condition of the Church of God when it is more sanctified in the future, and God dwells among them. They will then adore God in His holiness above any other attribute. Even God Himself seems to take pride in His holiness above any other attribute. Therefore, when God desires to elevate Himself in His glory and provide the highest revelation of Himself, He does so by emphasizing His holiness. Isaiah 57:15 says, "For thus saith the high and lofty one that inhabiteth eternity, whose name is holy." When God wants to exalt Himself, He emphasizes that His name is holy. So, when God wanted to swear by Himself (Amos 4:2), He swore by His holiness. Just as the Scripture says, when God could swear by no one greater, He swore by Himself, I can also say that when God could swear by no excellence greater than this, He swore by His holiness.

Again, God glorifies heaven itself as the abode of His holiness. Heaven is the dwelling place of God's glory, where God fully manifests His glory. But what is that glory? It is the pinnacle of all, the holiness of God. Isaiah 63:15 says, "Look down from heaven and behold from the habitation of thy holiness and thy glory." Even the throne of God is a throne of holiness, as Psalm 47:8 states, "God sitteth upon the throne of his holiness." Just as kings are elevated and exalted on their thrones, God is exalted on the throne of His holiness. Solomon made himself a throne of ivory and overlaid it with the finest gold (1 Kings 10:18). But God's throne is a throne of holiness, a throne radiating bright holiness.

Furthermore, when God rejoices in His people, He does so because they are a holy people. Deuteronomy 7:6 states, "For thou art a holy people unto the Lord thy God: the Lord thy God hath chosen thee to be a peculiar people unto himself above all the people that are upon the face of the earth." Moreover, you will find that this attribute of holiness is more specifically ascribed to the third person in the Trinity. While God the Father is a holy God and the Son is the Holy One of God, the Holy Spirit derives His name from holiness. It is worth noting that all three persons claim an equal share in the work of holiness in the creature, as holiness is such an integral part of God's glory that all three persons work it wherever it is found. The Father is a Sanctifier, as Jude mentions in the first verse of his Epistle, "To them that are sanctified by God the Father." Concerning the Son, Ephesians 5:25-26 states, "Husbands, love your wives, even as Christ also loved the Church, and gave himself for it, that he might sanctify and cleanse it with the washing of water by the Word." Christ gave Himself for His Church not only to bring it to Heaven but also to sanctify it. As for the Spirit of God, 1 Corinthians 6:11 mentions, "And such were some of you: but ye are washed, but ye are sanctified, but ye are justified, in the Name of the Lord Jesus, and by the Spirit of our God." Therefore, all three persons are involved in this work. This is the glorious work of the Father, Son, and Holy Spirit.

Furthermore, holiness must undoubtedly be the glory of God because it is the highest perfection and rectitude of an intelligent free Agent. An intelligent free Agent is the highest being of all, and holiness represents the righteousness of that being, making it inherently glorious. This is why grace is referred to as God's image because it reflects God's highest excellence. An image properly represents another thing by highlighting its excellence. If it does so in a common and general manner, it is not a true image of it. In Scripture, holiness is also referred to as the beauty of God, as seen in Psalm 27:4, "One thing have I desired of the Lord, that I will seek after, that I may dwell in the house of the Lord all the days of my life, to behold the beauty of the Lord, and to inquire in his Temple." God's beauty is His holiness, which is revealed in His ordinances and worship. Psalm 110:3 refers to the ordinances as the "beauty of holiness": "Thy people shall be willing in the day of thy power in the beauties of holiness." Even the beginnings of holiness in the hearts of Saints are called the glory of God, as in Romans 3:23, "All have sinned and come short of the glory of God." This implies that the very initial work of holiness in the hearts of believers is called the glory of God, much more so His infinite holiness. Furthermore, holiness enhances all the other attributes of God and makes them glorious and honorable, as Psalm 111:9 states, "Holy and reverend is his name." God's name is revered because it is holy. Therefore, regardless of how excellent the attributes of God may be, if you can conceive of them being separated from His holiness, they do not render His name revered. This underscores the vital importance of striving for holiness. If all the excellencies of God cannot render His name revered when separated from holiness, then no matter what excellence a creature possesses in terms of abilities, wealth, worldly status, dignity, and honour, without holiness, you cannot rightfully say that God's name is revered. Instead, you must say, "Holy and reverend is his name," as it is said of God, whose name is revered because He is holy.

Again, God's name is glorious through holiness because it is the ultimate purpose of all His works to promote holiness. Just as a skilled craftsman showcases artistry in the beginning of his work and demonstrates the excellence of his craftsmanship at its culmination, so it is with God. God desires to be honored in all His creative and providential works, but at the pinnacle of His work, His ultimate aim is to be honored as a holy God and to have a holy people who will honor Him both in this world and for all eternity. Holiness is what God sought to achieve in the creation of heaven and earth, and it is His goal in all His providential ways. It is the primary purpose for which the Son of God came into the world – to redeem a people who would serve Him in holiness. Holiness is also the end of God's grand plan from all eternity. Furthermore, God aims to manifest the beauty of His holiness in two great attributes, Mercy and Justice, which are the manifestations of His holiness. He desires to make these attributes shine for all eternity. This is the purpose God strives for, and therefore holiness must indeed be the glory of God's name.

Now, a little on the third point: Why is this title, "glorious in holiness," given to God in this Song of Moses? The reason is to demonstrate that the infinite excellence of God's power is such that it is exercised without any admixture of the slightest evil. In this act of mighty power, God exhibited His infinite holiness. This sets God apart from humanity. It is exceedingly difficult for a person to perform great deeds and demonstrate great power without a mixture of evil. It is akin to the behavior of water: when it flows shallow, it may remain clear, but when it rises and overflows, it becomes muddy, often carrying a significant amount of impurities with it. Although in everyday and ordinary tasks, people may not reveal their impurity, it is rare that they do not display a considerable amount of filthiness when they attempt to accomplish great things. However, this is not the case with God. God is great in power and retains the glory of His holiness. Even when God demonstrated His immense wrath against His enemies, the glory of His holiness remained. This is a remarkable distinction from humans. When individuals become angry, they often reveal a great deal of impurity. Many people who appear exceedingly gentle and loving when they are pleased can quickly display an abundance of filthiness when provoked. This is comparable to a pond that may seem clear on the surface but is full of mud at the bottom. Stir it even slightly, and the water becomes nothing but filth. Parents, for example, may struggle to express displeasure or correct their children without exposing a great deal of corruption accompanying their anger. The same is true for those in positions of authority and servants. When executing justice on others, self-interest and self-centered motives often taint their actions. However, the glory of God lies in the fact that when He reveals His wrath, even though it is severe, He remains glorious in holiness. He is infinitely powerful in His wrath and in the execution of His judgments while maintaining infinite holiness. This is why the vials of God's wrath are described as being made of gold, the purest metal, symbolizing the purity of God in executing His judgments. Let us strive to emulate God in this regard. If you have a passionate spirit and are easily provoked, revealing an abundance of filthiness, consider how unlike God you are. Even when you must express displeasure with sin or correct your children and servants, ensure that holiness remains the essence of your corrective actions, for it is the beauty that should accompany all correction.

Again, this title is attributed to God here because in this monumental work, He manifested His faithfulness in fulfilling His promises to His people. God had made numerous promises to His Church regarding their preservation and deliverance, and in this instance, God fulfilled these promises. God's faithfulness is an aspect of His holiness; therefore, Moses and the people praised His name using the title "glorious in holiness." It is noteworthy and highly beneficial for us to understand that God's faithfulness is a facet of His holiness. A comparison of two Scriptures highlights this: Isaiah 55:3 says, "I will make an everlasting covenant with you, even the sure mercies of David," and this verse is quoted in Acts 13:34 as, "I will give you the sure mercies of David." However, in the original text, it reads, "the holy and faithful things of David." When God demonstrates mercy according to His word, He reveals the glory of His holiness. This understanding of God's holiness and faithfulness serves to strengthen the faith of God's people. As you have heard, the glory of God is His holiness, and one component of His holiness is His faithfulness in fulfilling His promises to His people. Therefore, it is crucial for God, who loves His own glory, to be faithful in keeping His promises, and God regards it as His glory to do so. While your comfort and preservation are precious to you, God's glory is even dearer to Him. In fact, God's glory is more precious to Him than your soul or your eternal destiny could ever be to you. The pinnacle of God's glory is His holiness, and His holiness is defined by one thing: His faithfulness to His promises.

Now, for the application of this, first: consider whether you have truly comprehended God or not. Allow me to pose this question: What is the aspect of God's excellence that captivates your soul? We often speak of God's excellence, claiming to love Him, delight in Him, and bless Him. However, what is it about God that draws your heart towards Him and causes your soul to genuinely love, bless, and delight in Him, as you profess? Is it merely that God will show you mercy, pardon your sins, save your soul, and bring you to heaven? While these are certainly reasons to love and bless God, there must be more. It is the very person of God Himself that must capture your heart, and it must be the person of God in His excellence. What is that excellence? It is His holiness. Has the radiance of God's infinite holiness ever shone upon your heart, drawing your heart toward God and prompting you to stand in adoration and amazement? Has your heart leaped with joy upon beholding the brilliance of His holiness, and do you love Him for this reason? If so, then you have truly understood God, and your heart has been genuinely drawn to Him. As David expressed in Psalm 119:140, "Your word is very pure; therefore your servant loves it." Can you say, "O Lord, you are pure, you are holy; therefore, your servant loves you"? Do you love His holy word, His holy worship, His holy servants, His holy ordinances, and all holy things because of the beauty of His holiness? If the beauty of God's holiness is what draws your heart in love toward God, then proportionately, it will be the beauty of holiness in all things that are holy that draws your heart to love and delight in them. You will regard His saints as glorious in holiness, and you will see His worship, His word, and His ordinances as glorious in holiness, leading your heart to be drawn towards them. In Psalm 33:21, you can observe how the saints of God rejoiced in the Lord and had their hearts drawn to Him because of His holiness. Their hearts rejoiced in Him because they had trusted in His holy name. Trusting in God's holy name is what causes our hearts to rejoice in Him.

Secondly, the people of God should find great comfort in dealing with Him as a holy God, even though they encounter much unholiness in the people with whom they interact. In God, there is nothing but holiness, and indeed, the very beauty and glory of holiness. It is a delightful and rare blessing to meet a friend who possesses a pure and clean heart, one free from any mixture, who has holy intentions and a spirit without deceit. The joy is immense when two friends with such pure hearts meet and are in agreement. Yet, how much greater is the delight when you meet with God, in whom there is no mixture whatsoever! God delights in us, even though we possess only fragments of His holiness. How much more should we rejoice in Him who is infinite in holiness? When dealing with humans, our expectations are often disappointed. We may encounter individuals with exceptional talents and gifts, but when we engage with them, we find that their character and spirits do not match the excellence of their gifts. This can be deeply vexing to the saints. However, take solace in the fact that when you deal with God, you will find nothing but holiness in Him. He always acts in accordance with His excellence. As I previously mentioned, this is the nature of God's holiness – it is the perfection of His will, ensuring that He works in harmony with His eminence and excellence. While humans may possess excellence but not always grace in their hearts to act in accordance with it, God always works in alignment with His eminence and excellence. When our hearts are elevated by the sight of God's excellence and we know that we will always find Him acting in accordance with it, what a comforting thought this is for a gracious soul, despite all the evil encountered among the people with whom they interact.

Furthermore, for the comfort of the saints, if God is glorious in holiness (as in the previous point, since there is none like God, there is none like His people), then the saints are also glorious in holiness. What makes an infinite God glorious must certainly make a humble human being a glorious creature. While it is true that what brings glory to a poor man may not bring glory to a king, what brings glory to a king will certainly bring glory to a beggar. Holiness bestows a radiance and glory upon the divine nature itself, upon the infinite God. So, if you possess holiness, it must inevitably bestow glory upon you. It is worth noting that the impartation of God's holiness to us is expressed differently than when He imparts any other attribute to us. When God imparts His knowledge to us, we are not said to partake of the divine nature because of it, nor when He imparts His power, and so on. However, when God imparts His holiness to us, we are said to become partakers of the divine nature. The holiness of the saints is essentially a reflection of God's holiness, like a beam of His holiness. As the Scripture says in Hebrews 12:10, "He chastens us for our profit, that we might be partakers of his holiness." Note, "His holiness." Therefore, it bestows remarkable glory and excellence upon us because it enables us to work as God does and to live as God lives. What is God's holiness, as mentioned before, but that by which He works for Himself as His ultimate end, in accordance with His own excellence? The saints, to the extent of their capacity, come to work for God as their ultimate end, in accordance with the infinite excellence of God Himself. Consequently, they live as God lives and work as God works, thus making them suitable for communion with God. In communion, there must be the same life, and no creature can have communion with God unless they live the same life as God does. But if you partake of holiness, you live the life that God lives and are thus qualified to have communion with God Himself.

Furthermore, holiness not only brings glory to your person but also sanctifies everything you have and do. It consecrates all aspects of your life, just as gold was sanctified by the altar. Even your natural actions and the events of God's common providence become sanctified for God's people. There is a radiance on all the good they enjoy because of the holiness that God has instilled in them. Just as God's holiness bestows radiance on all His attributes, holiness in the saints enhances their abilities, reputation, possessions, and interactions with others. Holiness imparts beauty to every aspect of their lives. Consider a person with exceptional natural abilities; if they lack holiness, there is no radiance or beauty in them. However, take someone with talented abilities and holiness, and the radiance that emanates from them is remarkable.

Moreover, holiness is the very essence of eternal life, the starting point of eternal life in the heart, and something that will undoubtedly mature into eternal life. Holiness is also the specific object of God's delight. God takes pleasure not in a person's physical attributes but in their holiness. Regardless of a person's background, if God perceives any trace of holiness in them, His soul will be drawn to that individual.

Additionally, holiness signifies the separation of the creature for God and eternal life. There are two types of separation of a creature for God: passive and active. Psalm 4:3 states, "The Lord hath set apart him that is godly for himself," signifying a passive separation. However, holiness also involves an active principle by which individuals set themselves apart for God. In His eternal election, God sets apart those He intends to save for Himself, declaring, "These are the ones I have chosen from the common mass of humanity to showcase the riches of My grace and to dwell with Me for all eternity." If God were to proclaim from heaven that He had set apart a man or woman from eternity to glorify them with Himself forever, everyone would regard such individuals as truly glorious creatures. But know this: if God has imprinted the image of His holiness upon you, you receive as much honour from God as if He had made such a declaration to you, and in some respects, even more. For when God has implanted a principle of His own Spirit within you, enabling you to consecrate yourself and your entire being to God, this is a higher level of honour. In the former case, you are passive, whereas in the latter, you are active. Conversely, there is more dreadful evil in unholiness than in reprobation. People fear reprobation, where God sets them apart from eternity to display the glory of His justice upon them, and rightfully so, as it is terrifying. However, while you may find this terrifying, you are actively involved in something even more dreadful. That is, through the impurity and wickedness of your heart and actions, you actively set yourself apart for eternal wrath and misery. Reprobation is passive; you are merely set apart. In contrast, sin involves an active separation from God to eternal misery. I intended to further explore the comparison between the glory and happiness of the saints and the misery of the wicked, but time does not permit.

Furthermore, just as holiness confers reverence upon the name of God, holiness in the saints commands a respectful regard for them in the very consciences of wicked individuals. Even the most wicked among men, despite their complaints about you, should recognize that if you lead a strict and devout life, your close walk with God will earn respect and reverence from their hearts, despite their inner resistance. The reason why the people of God often fail to gain respect and esteem is that they do not maintain strictness in their conduct. Many people misunderstand this concept: they believe that strictness is disregarded and scorned, so they begin to compromise and slacken in their commitment to exacting standards. However, this only leads to their diminished respect. In the eyes of God, this outcome is just. Does relaxing your commitment to holiness help you gain a more reverential respect? No, it is by walking even closer with God that you will earn respect in the consciences of others. Despite their best efforts, you will challenge their desires but convince their consciences. Even in their most serious moments, they will wish to be in your position, often expressing this sentiment on their deathbeds. Holiness imparts excellence and glory to humble and ordinary things.

Consider the Law, which elevated a simple piece of wood, leather, or brass when consecrated for a holy purpose. This transformation was initiated by God, not by humans. It is a great mistake for anyone to think that they have the power to make God esteem a creature more highly than He has ordained. It would be audacious for me to assert that common stones, through my will, should be considered holy and consecrated to God, rendering them untouchable. This would involve attributing a divine excellence to something that possesses only natural qualities. However, when God's ordinance is involved, true glory is bestowed upon it. In the case of the Temple, every component, including the wood and brass, was considered excellent because it was dedicated to God through divine institution. I would argue as follows: if ceremonial holiness can elevate a piece of leather in such a manner, then what kind of glory must the image of God bestow upon an immortal soul!

A further point to consider is this: if God is glorious in holiness, then certainly (brethren) God will uphold holiness in the world. This is one reason, among others, for this Title given to God here, because He worked for His Church: God will honour His own Ordinances and worship, and will preserve His Saints who are holy. "Preserve me, O Lord," says David, "for I am holy; and You will not give Your holy one to see corruption." If you are God's holy one, He will not abandon you to the power of corruption; He will defend and uphold you. Therefore, the Psalmist says in Psalm 68:35, "O God, You are terrible out of Your holy places." Will anyone harm God's people when they are in the place of His holy worship? God will be terrible to those who oppose His people; these expressions are against God's enemies because they oppose the holiness of God and the holiness of His people. Let all people be cautious when opposing the Saints and the ways of God's holy worship; for God will uphold holiness. Therefore, it is our responsibility to honour holiness ourselves and to promote the glory of God's holiness as much as we can in the world. Let us all strive to be holy, as our heavenly Father is holy.

Let that be our prayer, as in Psalm 90:17, "Let the beauty of the Lord our God be upon us." Grow in holiness, which is the beauty of God; spend much time in communion with God, so that you may become holy. When Moses spent forty days on the mountain conversing with God, he came down with his face shining. Certainly, those who have much communion with God will have faces shining with holiness. There is much to gain from conversing with God, who is a holy God. Display the beauty of holiness in your conduct so that others may say, "If one beam of holiness is so delightful in such a man or woman, O how glorious in holiness God Himself must be!" I recall what a heathen said about the God of the Christians when he saw their courage: "Certainly," he said, "the God of the Christians is a great God." Let us live so holily before others that they may see holiness in our conduct and be compelled to acknowledge that the God of this people is a holy God. Above all, examine your heart to cleanse it when you draw near to this holy God in holy worship. Be mindful of your steps; do not come into the presence of such a holy God in a state of uncleanness. Consider the notable expression in Joshua 24:19 when the people declared their intention to serve the Lord: "You cannot serve the Lord," Joshua said, "for He is a holy God." He implied that serving the Lord was more serious than they thought because they were dealing with a holy God, and external worship alone would not suffice. People do not truly know God when they treat His service so lightly; if they truly beheld God's holiness, they would regard His service as a weighty matter. "Who can stand before this holy God?" as they said in 1 Samuel 6:20. If you truly apprehend God as a holy God, your heart will be filled with fear and awe, and you will ask, "Who can stand before this holy God?" In the assembly of the Saints, God is greatly to be feared and revered by all who are around Him (Psalm 89:7). But if you draw near to Him, you must strive to sanctify your hearts. How can you come before the radiance and beauty of God's holiness with a willfully unclean heart? The passage in Job 13:11 is very

noteworthy: "Shall not His excellency make you afraid?" You have heard
that God's holiness is His excellency. Now I ask you, when you have
to deal with Him, shall not His excellency make you afraid? Are you
conscious of your uncleanness and yet approach a holy God without
fear and trembling? It is audacious to have such a bold and daring heart
that can come into the presence of a holy God with an unholy heart
without trembling. In all our dealings with God, it would be immensely
beneficial to have a clear understanding of His holiness.

Again, strive to exalt God in this manner: just as God is glorious in
holiness, display His glory by preserving the purity of His worship. It is of
great importance to God that we are cautious not to defile His worship.
God's Ordinances represent the beauty of His holiness, so we must
endeavour to approach them in purity and cleanliness. God commands
His Church to keep the vessels of His sanctuary holy, which refers to
the ordinances. We are negligent in our duty if we do not maintain the
holiness of the ordinances. In Exodus 20:24-25, God instructs them to
build an altar: "If you make an altar of stone for me, do not build it with
dressed stones, for you will defile it if you use a tool on it." They might
have wondered, "Shall we have an altar made of uncut stone? Shouldn't
we polish and make it exquisite and sumptuous? Wouldn't that make it
more appealing?" God's response is clear: "No, if you use a tool on it, you
will defile it." We often mistakenly believe that certain mixtures of men
and various ceremonies would enhance the glory of God's worship. This
is a grave error. It's like prostitutes who paint their faces, not content
with their natural beauty, adorning themselves more lavishly than chaste
matrons. This is akin to the harlotry of Babylon: how splendid is their
worship, and how they strive to captivate the senses with their outward
displays, yet they lack the purity of God's worship. These things indeed
defile the worship of God. Compare two passages on this matter: Isaiah
44:9 states, "All who make idols are nothing, and the things they treasure
are worthless." These images are considered delightful by idolaters, but

God calls them worthless. In contrast, Ezekiel 7:20 says, "They took pride in their beautiful jewelry and used it to make their detestable idols." They cherished these items as beautiful, but God regarded them as detestable. In contrast, when God speaks of His own ordinances, He says, "As for the beauty of its ornament, it majestically displays His holiness." What powerful expressions! This is God's worship. If we introduce anything of our own into God's worship, it is detestable to Him. Therefore, if we wish to honour and glorify God in His holiness, let us keep His worship pure, for holiness befits God's worship forever.

Moreover, contemplating this should humble us and cause us to be ashamed of the remaining unholiness in our hearts. The vision of God's holiness made Isaiah cry out in Isaiah 6:5, "Woe to me! I am ruined! For I am a man of unclean lips, and I live among a people of unclean lips, and my eyes have seen the King, the Lord Almighty." Surely, there is nothing in the world as powerful in humbling the heart as the holiness of God. Your heart is genuinely humbled for sin when you view it as that which is contrary to the pure nature of God. You are not troubled by your sin solely out of fear that it will lead to hell, but also because you have glimpsed the infinite holiness and purity of God's nature. You are deeply affected by the contrast between your own sinful nature and God's infinite holiness. Examine your hearts by this measure to determine if your humility is genuine. It is a strong argument when the infinite holiness of God has caused you to recognise your uncleanness and, as a result, has humbled you.

Lastly, we all have a tremendous need for Jesus Christ! If God is glorious in holiness, then every one of us should acknowledge, "Who can stand before such a holy God!" If it were not for the holiness of the blessed mediator who stands between the Father and us, presenting His infinite satisfaction to the Father for our sins and clothing us in His righteousness, woe to us! Imagine that all the excellencies of heaven and earth were combined in one creature, except holiness. Even if that creature had the tiniest trace of uncleanness and unholiness, God would eternally detest that creature. If there were no mediator between that creature and God, God's wrath would be unleashed upon it eternally. God's holiness is so glorious that He infinitely abhors filthiness. We may be astonished to hear of such great misery threatened to wicked individuals, but our wonder would cease if we truly understood God's holiness. God so intensely despises sin that He instantly cast down all the angels who fell into chains of eternal darkness. He refused to engage in the slightest dialogue with them or to reconcile with them forever. Now, what is the reason that, despite our inherent uncleanness, God is pleased to be reconciled to us, welcome us into His presence, and grant us hope to see His face with joy for all eternity? The reason is this: we have a mediator, and they do not. Were it not for that mediator, even if we wept streams of blood from our eyes, God would still hate and abhor us, and His wrath would eternally consume us. Therefore, while you may rejoice in your inherent holiness, set your hearts primarily on the perfect holiness of Jesus Christ and present it to God. Though you may have much uncleanness in yourself and in your deeds (for what is our offering of duty to the holy God?), take comfort in this: you do not approach God on your own but through Christ. In Him, you have the freedom to come and may confidently gaze upon God's face. This is the great mystery of godliness revealed in the Gospel: despite the infinite holiness of God, there is a way for us polluted creatures to joyfully behold this God. This mystery is exclusively taught in the Gospel. While people may believe they can approach God and cry out for mercy now, in the future, when God reveals the brilliance of His holiness to you and you come to realize your uncleanness, your heart will sink into eternal despair. You will be unable to bear the sight of God then. If you are not acquainted with God through this path of reconciliation, you are eternally lost. Therefore, study the Gospel's mystery and make use of Christ so that the glory of God's holiness may be your comfort, not your terror.

This sermon was preached on March 21, 1640.

But Christ is all in all.

Christ is all in all. – Colossians 3:11

I t is not long since (as some of you may remember) that in this place, the subject was discussed about the saints' enjoyment of God, to be all in all, from 1 Corinthians 15:28. And then I told you that we had such an expression in Scripture but only twice: applied to God in the happiness of the saints' enjoyment of Him in heaven, and applied here to Christ, of what Christ is to them for the present. That which was discussed about God being all in all is the end; this that is to be delivered concerning Christ being all in all is that which brings the soul to that blessed end. Wherefore then, as Christ Himself says, John 14:1, "Ye believe in God, believe also in me." So I say, as God shall be all in all eternally to the saints, do you believe in that? Believe also in this, that I am to deliver to you this day, that Christ, He is all and in all.

The Apostle Saint Paul was a chosen vessel to bear the name of Christ, to carry it up and down in the world: and indeed, his spirit was full of Christ; he desired to know nothing but Christ, to preach nothing but Christ, to be found in none but Christ; the very name of Christ was delightful to him. He seeks in all his Epistles to magnify Christ, and in these words (that I have read unto you), he does magnify Christ; he makes Him not only great but makes Him all. There is neither Greek nor Jew, circumcision nor uncircumcision, Barbarian, Scythian, bond nor free, but Christ is all and in all: that is, there is no privilege in the one to commend them to God, and no lack of anything in the other to hinder them from God; let men be what they will in their outward respects, what is that to God? Let them be never so mean in regard to all outwards, that cannot hinder them from the enjoyment of God. For God looks not at these things, but Christ is all and in all to them; so far as God sees Christ in any, He accepts them: if Christ be not there, whatever they have, He regards them not. Christ is all in all, even in the esteem of the Father Himself: He was the delight of the Father from all eternity, Proverbs 8:30, and the Father took infinite contentment in Him upon His willingness to undertake this blessed work of the redemption of mankind. God the Father is infinitely satisfied in Christ; He is all in all to Him. Surely, if Christ is an object sufficient for the satisfaction of the Father, much more then is He an object sufficient for the satisfaction of any soul.

But that which is the main scope here of the Holy Ghost in this high expression of Christ's transcendent excellency (that I may come presently to it), I shall deliver it in this doctrinal proposition: That Christ is the only means of conveyance of all good that God the Father intends to communicate unto the children of men, in order to eternal life; He is all and in all. This that I am now to preach unto you, namely, God's communicating of Himself in His mercy to mankind, through a mediator, it is the very sum of the Gospel, the great mystery of godliness. It is the chief part of the mind and counsel of God, that He would have made known to the children of men in this world. This is the great embassage that the ministers of the Gospel have to bring unto the sons and daughters of men, and it is the most absolutely necessary point in all Divinity.

I suppose that upon first hearing this, everyone acknowledges its truth. You will say, "It's true; we can have no good from God except in and through Christ." Well, there is much significance in what you say when you affirm that all must come from God in Christ. In all your prayers and petitions, you usually conclude them with "through Jesus Christ." However, often this is spoken without fully grasping the glory of God contained in such an expression. What I shall strive to do today is to reveal to you some of the glory of God shining in the truth that God communicates Himself through a mediator, through His Son. This is a crucial point of theology that is absolutely necessary to know for eternal life. It is possible to be ignorant of many other truths and still be saved, but there must be some knowledge of this, or there can be no salvation. Misunderstanding this very thing is the downfall and eternal undoing of countless souls. Many believe that they need and can only be saved by God's mercy, a conviction that even the light of nature can instill. But that God communicates His mercy through a mediator, this they are unaware of, and they fail to grasp the reality of this truth. As a result, they perish eternally, praying to God for mercy but not coming to Him through a mediator. This is the essence of the Gospel and the most supernatural truth revealed in the entire Bible. It is a truth that remained hidden from much of the world for many ages. Scripture states that "the Princes of the world knew it not." It is a truth that we cannot comprehend through the light of nature. In 1 Corinthians 1:21, we read, "The world by wisdom knew not God," meaning that by all their arts, sciences, and natural wisdom, they did not truly know God; they did not know God in Christ. There are no traces of this truth in all the works of creation or providence. Thus, in Ephesians 3:8, Saint Paul says he was appointed to preach the unsearchable riches of Christ. These riches have no traces; that's the meaning of the word "unsearchable." There are no traces of the riches of the Gospel in creation. Therefore, you cannot discover it there. While many other religious points have traces in creation, and much can be discerned about God through the light of nature – such as the idea that all our good comes from communion with God, that when we have offended God, we must seek His pardon and mercy – the fact that God communicates Himself through Christ, and that not one drop of mercy concerning eternal life can come from God except through Christ the mediator, not a single trace of this truth is found in all of God's works.

This is what is so supernatural that it surpasses perfect nature. Adam knew nothing of this in his perfect state. Yes, this is what the angels themselves desire to investigate, considering it a profound mystery. In 1 Peter 1:12, it is stated that the angels "stoop down" (for that is the meaning of the word) as if to peer into a deep pit. Imagine something lying in a deep pit, and when someone wants to see it, they bend down with their bodies to peer into the pit; that is the essence of the word. So the angels perceive a profound depth in the mystery of the Gospel, and they stoop down to examine it, seeking to understand what it entails. Furthermore, this requires a work of the Spirit that goes beyond the ordinary work of the Spirit of God to reveal it to the soul. In 1 Corinthians 2:10, when addressing the mystery of the Gospel, the Apostle says, "The Spirit that searcheth the deep things of God," reveals this; it is the extraordinary work of the Spirit of God, as He searches the deep things of God, that discloses this truth to us. Therefore, since it is so, it should not be taken lightly. You might say, "It is true; all must come through Jesus Christ." Well, you see a glimpse of it initially, but there is much more to this truth than we realise. This truth is the most beneficial of all the truths found in the Bible. There is no growth in godliness until we come to know God in Christ. Knowledge of God provides something to work on the heart, and many struggle against their sin because they see it as against God's law and engage in duties because God requires them, which is commendable. However, until they genuinely understand the mystery of the Gospel, of God revealing Himself to His people through

a mediator, they fumble in their pursuit of godliness; they do not thrive
and grow in it. Thus, Christians living under a ministry where, despite
receiving many good truths, they have little understanding of the mystery
of Christ as the mediator, their Christian walk remains shallow, and they
do not sanctify God in their conduct. I recall a statement by Erasmus
when he was urged to write against Luther, with the promise of a great
bishopric as a reward. He replied, "Luther is greater than I can argue
against, for I have learned more from one small page of Luther than from
the entire work of Thomas Aquinas, the great Scholastic theologian."
Therefore, understanding even one truth, one sentence about the mystery of the Gospel, in this manner of God's self-communication through
Christ, instructs the soul and causes it to thrive and grow in godliness
far more than thousands of sermons on mere moral principles. There is
an excellent passage that illustrates this in Ephesians 3:17 and beyond,
"That Christ may dwell in your hearts by faith, that ye being rooted and
grounded in love, may be able to comprehend with all saints what is the
breadth, and length, and depth, and height, and to know the love of
Christ, which passeth knowledge." Note what follows, "That ye might
be filled with all the fullness of God" (verse 19). By coming to know God
in Christ, that is, understanding that Christ is the means by which God
communicates Himself to us, we become filled with all the fullness of
God. Many Christians have spiritually impoverished and empty hearts
because they know so little of God in Christ within this mystery of the
Gospel.

Lastly, there is no truth revealed in all the Scriptures by which we can
honour God as much as by this one. Indeed, this is the greatest honour
that God desires in the world—to be honoured in His Son and in the
grand design He has of bringing forth glorious things through His Son.
Therefore, even if we know a great deal about God and wish to honour
Him solely as the Creator of heaven and earth, God does not accept
that honour; it is merely honouring Him in a natural way. We do not

truly know how to honour God correctly, so as to be accepted by Him, until we come to honour Him in an Evangelical way, to honour Him in His Son. Yet, for the most part, even in the Church of God, many offer honour to Him merely in a natural way, rather than through this spiritual Evangelical service of God. Now you see the importance of this point; let us explore it.

First, I will demonstrate the truth of it in Scripture.

Second, I will explain how it is that no good can be communicated to us from God for eternal life except through Christ.

Third, I will elucidate how Christ becomes the means and conduit for all good from His Father to us.

Fourth, I will provide examples of some significant matters, great things in which most of God's goodness is conveyed to us, and demonstrate how in these matters, Christ is all in all to us.

Fifth, I will present the reasons why God has chosen this method of communicating Himself to us through His Son, why He does not communicate Himself to us directly, but through a mediator. These are the five aspects of the doctrinal part.

Regarding the first point, the Scripture consistently supports this notion, particularly in the New Testament. Consider the words of Christ in John 14:6: "I am the way, the truth and the life; no man cometh unto the Father but by me." It is clear that there is no approach to the Father except through Christ, and Christ is the way. In 1 Corinthians 3, towards the end of the chapter, the Apostle asserts, "All things are yours, whether Paul, or Apollos, or Cephas, or the world, or life, or death, or things present, or things to come; all are yours." How is this so? Note, "All are yours, and ye are Christ's, and Christ is God's." God the Father is the source of all goodness; everything primarily emanates from Him. However, it does not come directly from Him. He does not say, "All are yours because you belong to God, and therefore everything is yours." Instead, He says, "All are yours, and you belong to Christ, and Christ belongs to God." Thus, you can see how Christ intercedes between you and God.

All good resides in God; that is true. However, how can we partake in that goodness? There is such a vast separation between these two terms, "yours" and "God's," that if Christ were not in the middle, they would never unite. Christ's intervention and connection bring them together, and then all things are yours because you belong to Christ, and Christ belongs to God. To understand this better, consider God the Father as the source of all goodness and Christ as a cistern, and from Him, pipes are conveyed to every believer. Faith acts as the mouth that attaches to each pipe, drawing from God, but this goodness flows from God through Christ. The Father fills the Son with all goodness, and it reaches the soul of every believer through the Son by faith. Although this analogy may be too simplistic for the profound mystery we are about to explore, it conveys the Holy Spirit's intent.

We find another remarkable expression of this mystery in the Epistle to the Ephesians, particularly in chapters 2 and 3. In chapter 2, verse 12, after stating that they were once without hope and without God in the world, the Apostle goes on to say in verse 13, "But now in Christ Jesus ye who sometimes were far off are made nigh by the blood of Christ." It is through the blood of Christ that you have any connection with God. Ephesians 3:12 continues to elucidate this truth, stating, "In whom we have boldness and access with confidence by the faith of him." Here, "in whom" refers to Christ. In Christ, we gain boldness and access to God. "Boldness" implies the freedom to speak openly before God, and "access" refers to being led by the hand of Christ to the Father. There is no approach to the Father except through Christ, and Christ takes a believer by the hand and leads them to the Father, granting them boldness. It is as if a traitor were banished from the court and the prince, serving as a mediator, took the traitor by the hand, saying, "Come, I will lead you to my father. Though you have offended him, being in my hand, you need not fear, and you can go before him with boldness and confidence." This illustrates the meaning of the text: "In Christ, we have boldness and access with confidence." Although there was once a dreadful rift between the Father and us, being led by the hand of Christ grants us access and the freedom to speak. The truth is evident throughout the Gospel.

Now, if you wish to understand how it is that even though God, in His nature, is infinitely merciful and the fountain of all goodness, there seems to be an obstacle preventing even a single drop of this mercy from being communicated to humanity except through this specific way, let me explain. This situation arises due to the breach of the initial covenant God made with humanity. Only humans and angels, human and angelic natures, are capable of entering into a covenant with God, speaking of a covenant in the strict sense. Since they are capable of this way of interaction with God, God initially established a covenant with them and intended to convey and share His goodness with them through that covenant. However, since this covenant was broken, resulting in a rupture between God and humanity, there is a blockade due to that breach. Consequently, no goodness can now be obtained through the first covenant, which has been broken, and unless there is a second covenant, no goodness can be expected at all.

Furthermore, there exists an infinite gap between God and us, making it impossible for us to come together. This gap is not so much due to God's inherent excellence and our lowly status as it is due to the vastness of His holiness and our impurity and sinfulness; this is what creates the divide.

Additionally, there is the formidable influence of the law. The curse of the law hangs over every soul by default, acting as a barrier. The curse of the law is akin to a vessel sealed so tightly that not a drop of liquid can be poured into it. It stands between us and mercy, particularly as God views us merely in our natural state, without considering His Son.

Then, there are the demands of infinite Justice against humanity, which must be satisfied. Until Justice is appeased, mercy remains dormant unless it can provide satisfaction to Justice. So, when you consider these factors—the breach of the initial covenant, the chasm between God's holiness and human sinfulness, the grip of the curse of the law on humanity, and the cries of divine Justice that will not be silenced until satisfied—it becomes evident that receiving mercy from God is a distant possibility, despite Him being an infinite source of mercy. Unless there is an extraordinary means of conveying it to us, we remain far from receiving His mercy. We know from God's dealings with the fallen angels that there is no way to extend mercy to them; they are left to perish forever. If thousands of angels who fell from God were to cry out for mercy for thousands of thousands of years, they would not receive a single drop. Why? Because there is no mediator between God and them. Our fate would have been the same as theirs if there had not been a mediator between God and us. Many people think that if they acknowledge their sins and believe in God's infinite mercy, they will be fine. However, I must emphasize that even though God is infinitely merciful, if you have no connection to Christ, you may be lost forever.

But how is Christ all in all to us in God's communication of good to us?

The first foundation of all this is the covenant established by God the Father with His Son from all eternity. Therefore, in Titus 1:2, the Apostle speaks of "the promise of life which God, that cannot lie, promised before the world began." This promise can only refer to the covenant between the Father and the Son. Thus, the Apostle declares in 1 Corinthians 2:9-10, "Eye hath not seen, nor ear heard, neither have entered into the heart of man, the things which God hath prepared for them that love him. But God hath revealed them unto us by his Spirit." In this passage, the Spirit of God in the Gospel unveils the eternal thoughts and intentions of God concerning us, as well as the dealings between the Father and the Son regarding humanity before the world existed. With the covenant in place between the Father and the Son, and the Father's requirement within this covenant for satisfaction of infinite divine justice, Christ willingly complies with this requirement.

Therefore, in the second place, Christ becomes the means of conveyance by taking on our human nature. He makes us reconcilable to God by uniting human nature closely to the divine nature of the second person in the Trinity. This union results in only one person, a personal union, which is a profound mystery of the Gospel. There are two great mysteries in the Gospel: the first is the mystery of the Trinity, where there are several persons in one nature, and the second is the mystery of the hypostatic union, where there are multiple natures in one person. So, when Christ took human nature into such a close union with Himself, it was a significant preparation for God to consider peace with human nature rather than with the angels. Christ's humility in this act carries meritorious efficacy in the work of reconciling God to humanity, but it alone was not sufficient.

Therefore, in the third place, Christ willingly came into the world to become the head of a second covenant between God and humanity. He agreed to fulfill whatever God the Father required to satisfy divine Justice. Just as Adam, by being the head of the first covenant, was the means of conveying all evil to us, Christ, as the head of the second covenant, is the means of conveying all good to us. Through His submission, we receive all grace and mercy from God. This was the only way it could be, for if God had left it to us to fulfill the terms of the second covenant, we would have broken it just as we did the first. Christ, by becoming the head of the second covenant and performing everything required by the Father, including perfect obedience to the law and satisfaction to divine Justice, left divine Justice with nothing to charge against those whom Christ undertook to satisfy for. This was a powerful means by which God extended His grace and mercy to the souls of believers. What hinders the flow of His mercy? It is the curse of the law and the demands of divine Justice. However, Christ, by undertaking to bear that curse and satisfy divine Justice, restored as much honor to God through His suffering as was lost through human sin. Thus, human sin is compensated, and that is what Justice demands. Justice declares, "I have been dishonored by sin, and I must have this dishonor made up through suffering—suffering that restores as much honor as was lost through sin." These are the conditions upon which God will be reconciled to humanity, and on no other terms. Reflect on this, and you will understand the infinite necessity of Christ. God is with us on these terms: He says, "You have sinned against Me and dishonored Me. How do you propose to be delivered?" Humanity responds, "Lord, You are merciful." God affirms, "Yes, but I have resolved on this: I will receive as much honor through suffering as was lost through sinning." What would have become of us if we had been left to mend this breach ourselves? This is precisely why the damned in hell suffer eternally because they are there on these terms. God, being infinite, is dishonored, and they must remain there until God receives as much honor through their suffering as He lost through their sin. Even after thousands of years, the honor of God still demands more, and thus they must remain in hell forever. However, Christ, the great Savior, enters into a covenant with God, fulfills that covenant, and offers God a price that allows Him to regain as much honor through Christ's suffering for sin as was lost through the commission of sin. With this accomplished, the flow of mercy is unblocked, and the channels are opened. God, who is infinitely gracious and merciful in His nature, has created a glorious pathway for the streams of His mercy to flow freely to the children of men.

And consider this one particular aspect further, and then we shall conclude this section: In this, we can see that when God forgives sin and shows mercy to sinful creatures, He acts justly, not just mercifully. Therefore, the passage in Romans 3:25-26 is quite significant (a passage that troubled Martin Luther for a while regarding its meaning): "Whom God hath set forth to be a propitiation through faith in his blood, to declare his righteousness for the remission of sins that are past, through the forbearance of God; to declare, I say, at this time his righteousness, that he might be just, and the justifier of him which believeth in Jesus." This troubled Luther because it seemed strange that God would declare His righteousness in the forgiveness of sins. While everyone knows that God declares His mercy, the idea that God declares His righteousness, and that Christ is set as a propitiation for this purpose, may appear unusual. The Holy Ghost even repeats it, emphasizing, "To declare, I say, his righteousness." It's as if to say, consider that when God pardons sin, He not only reveals His grace and mercy but also proclaims His righteousness so that He may be considered just while justifying those who believe in Jesus. This illustrates the path Christ takes to be the means of conveying God's goodness to us—by fulfilling the covenant and thus satisfying divine Justice.

Lastly, He is the means of conveying good to us not only through His satisfaction but also through His intercession. He is now and forever seated at the right hand of the Father in glory, interceding for His people. He continually presents before the Father the work of His mediation, His merits, everything He has done and suffered, and pleads for the transmission of all necessary mercy and goodness to the souls and bodies of His redeemed people. It's as if He is eternally saying to the Father, "Father, behold here is my blood, my merits, my death, all my sufferings, the work of my humiliation. It is for these, yes, for this poor soul and that poor soul in particular." Christ does not only think of believers in a general sense but takes into account every individual believer. He continuously presents His infinite merits to the Father, pleading for the supply of all grace and mercy to us. Thus, He becomes an infinite conduit of good to the souls of His people, being all in all to them both in this life and for all eternity. That covers the third aspect—how Christ becomes the means of conveyance.

Now, let's move on to the fourth aspect: specific instances where we receive things from God and how Christ is everything in those matters. Firstly, consider the point of justification and the forgiveness of our sins, our acceptance as righteous. This is the primary need we have from God, and Christ is everything to us in this regard. It is the essence of the Gospel, as Romans 3:24 states, "Being justified freely by his grace, through the redemption that is in Jesus Christ." Luther had this to say about justification: "In matters of justification, Christ and faith must be solely paired together; they must be alone, with nothing else. But in our daily lives, good works come into play, just as it is between the bridegroom and the bride. In the bridal chamber, only the bridegroom and the bride are present. However, when they go out in public, they are accompanied by their attendants and servants. So, he compares justification to the bridal chamber—only Christ and faith must be there. But in our daily lives, all other graces accompany us, and good works come into play. But Christ is everything in this context."

First, it is not all we have done, nor even all that we can possibly do, that can justify us. You might think, "True, we have done very little at present." However, imagine that you could do your utmost in any aspect that God demands. You might hope that if you do your best, God will accept it. But you are greatly mistaken if you believe so. People often tend to view God as if the terms between God and themselves are simply this: God is merciful and compassionate, and though we are weak and can do very little, if we do our best, God will accept our intention as equivalent to the action. However, God does not accept mere intentions as deeds for justification. While it's true that, for those who are already justified, God accepts their intentions in the performance of duties and takes pleasure in them, in the matter of justification, particularly regarding the pardon of sin and acceptance as righteous, God requires perfect obedience. Despite all our efforts, unless we can present to God a perfect righteousness, we are eternally condemned. Even Abraham, Isaac, Jacob, David, Daniel, the Prophets, and the Apostles would have been lost forever if they did not possess a righteousness beyond their own. If they did not offer a perfect righteousness to their Father, all their righteousness would have been insufficient. Therefore, you should not rely on the belief that you are doing your best and have good intentions and desires. Even if all the righteousness of all the righteous individuals in the world were combined in one person, it would still be inadequate for their justification. You might argue that you can do very little by yourself, but if God enables you, then He will accept you. However, it's essential to understand that not even what God enables you to do can serve as the formality of your justification. The terms between God and you are such that nothing you can do on your own, or even with divine enablement, is accepted as your righteousness for eternal life.

Perhaps you'll say, "True, even with God's enablement, there may be imperfections, but God is merciful and will overlook them." To address this, I provide another consideration: it's not just about what you can do or what you can be enabled to do. Even if you consider God's mercy, when viewed merely as God's mercy to His creation and not in the context of Christ and the acceptance of a righteousness beyond your own, it cannot contribute to your justification. This is a common misconception. Many believe that their own abilities and actions, when combined with God's mercy, will suffice. They believe that when they have done something, God will then add His mercy to it as a supplement. However, it is not the combination of these factors that justifies you, especially when you view mercy from this perspective.

To clarify further, consider it this way: the role of God's mercy in justification is not to justify or make up for any deficiencies in your righteousness. Instead, the work of God's mercy in justifying a soul is to redirect that soul away from self-righteousness. It is to reveal to the soul its own unrighteousness and impurity. This is a significant and powerful work of God's mercy. I recall that Luther once said of himself that, during his time as a Papist, he was obedient out of conscience rather than for worldly gain or livelihood. But even so, he believed that what he considered to be gain was a loss. He did not consider it enough to act conscientiously and expect God's mercy to compensate for the rest. He had moved away from that perspective. Therefore, it is not the role of mercy to do this; instead, it unveils to the soul a higher form of righteousness—namely, the righteousness of the mediator, who is both God and man. It empowers the soul, through faith, to offer this righteousness to God the Father as satisfaction. This is the role of God's mercy in justification. Misunderstanding the role of God's mercy in influencing our justification can be extremely dangerous. We must be very cautious when it comes to this crucial point of justification, as everything hinges on it. I remember Luther saying that it is easy to declare that we embrace God's grace and the righteousness of Christ alone in matters of justification until the soul experiences a conflict. In times of troubled conscience, it becomes the most challenging thing in the world to do so. The people of God have certainly encountered this difficulty during times of troubled conscience. This covers the first aspect: Christ is everything in the matter of justification.

Secondly, he is all in all in the matter of adoption, as the Scripture affirms in Galatians 3:26, "For ye are all the children of God by faith in Christ Jesus," and in Galatians 4:4-5, "But when the fullness of the time was come, God sent forth his Son made of a woman, made under the law, to redeem them that were under the law, that we might receive the adoption of sons." Especially noteworthy is John 1:12, which states, "But as many as received him, to them he gave power to become the sons of God, even to them that believe on his name." The word translated as "power" in the Greek carries a deeper meaning—it signifies that he gave them authority to become the sons of God, not just the ability.

Many may lay claim to being children of God, but only those who are in Christ have the authority to claim it as their rightful status. If a stranger were to declare himself the King's son and heir to the Crown, he would be in grave danger because he is not truly the King's child. However, if someone is declared by an Act of Parliament to be the legitimate heir to the Crown, then he has the authority to make that claim. The same principle applies here: when we are in Christ, we gain the authority to assert our privilege of being the sons of God and heirs of heaven. This incredible privilege, which is far beyond our deserving, is granted to us in Christ, not only through the overflowing merit of his work but also through our union with him. We are joined to Christ in a profound way; we are spiritually wedded to him, united with his person, and thus become sons by virtue of his sonship. Consequently, we are the sons of God in a higher sense than the Angels, who are sons by creation. We, on the other hand, are the sons of God in Christ, through our mystical union with him. Christ is the Son of God, the second person in the Trinity, and through our union with him, we also become sons of God. In this aspect, Christ is all in all.

Furthermore, in terms of reconciliation and peace with God, Christ is all in all. Romans 5:1 declares, "Being justified by faith, we have peace with God through our Lord Jesus Christ." No amount of created power in heaven and earth can bring true peace to a troubled soul. There is no balm for a wounded spirit other than the application of the blood of Christ. He alone is the brazen Serpent capable of healing the wounds of a troubled conscience. As Luther aptly puts it, bringing comfort to an afflicted conscience is a more challenging task than raising the dead. Many fail to comprehend why some individuals are so troubled in their consciences. However, I must emphasize that were it not for a mighty redeemer, the conscience of a person who apprehends the wrath of God against them could never find peace. Thus, Christ is all in all in this matter of reconciliation and peace with God.

And so He is all in all in the matter of all our sanctification, specifically sanctification leading to eternal life. The Scripture mentions a general type of sanctification that, in some way, emanates from Christ. However, I am referring to the sanctification that pertains to our spiritual life. As you are aware, the Scripture states in John 3:36, "He that believeth on the Son hath everlasting life," and in John 1:16, "And of his fullness have all we received, and grace for grace." The fullness of Christ is imparted into the soul, so our sanctification is not merely meritorious but also efficient. Furthermore, it is to some extent material, for not only does He merit it and work it through His Spirit, but through our union with Him, sanctification flows into us as the very principle of our life. Just as blood flows from the liver into all parts of the body, through our union with Christ, sanctification flows into the souls of the Saints. In this case, sanctification does not primarily result from their striving, efforts, vows, or resolutions; rather, it flows to them through their embrace of Christ and their union with Him. A great deal of striving and endeavouring may prove entirely ineffective if it lacks recourse to Christ as the source and fount of all grace and holiness. I recall a German divine who admitted that before he grasped the grace of Christ in the Gospel, he made countless vows and covenants but could never overcome his corruptions. It was only when he understood that God's grace flows through Christ that he gained strength against them. The reason we often fail in sanctification is that we attempt to achieve it solely through our own efforts. The more effective approach is to have faith in Christ, and then life and grace will flow into the soul. While many moralities can be attained through natural light and the remnants of that light within us, they do not constitute sanctification leading to eternal life. That is why the sanctification of the Saints possesses such beauty and glory, as Christ is all in all in it. It is also why it carries immense power and strength, deriving from the strength of Christ, for He is all in all in it. Consequently, it is of a lasting nature and an immortal seed, exceeding the nature of Adam's innocence, which was lost but cannot be lost here, all because Christ is all in all in it. Thus, Christ is all in our sanctification as well.

Moreover, He is all in all in times of need, regardless of what we lack. Whether it is grace, gifts, or worldly comforts that we lack, Christ is sufficient. He stands in place of all these things, surpassing them all, and He will provide all in due time. Those who know Christ and have a relationship with Him can draw upon Him for supply, even if they experience the loss of various comforts. They possess the skill, art, and mystery of godliness, allowing them to make Christ all in all in times of need. Understanding how to find fullness in Christ when everything else is lacking is a profound skill and mystery of godliness.

Again, Christ is everything to the Saints in the enjoyment of all things. Even when they partake of creature comforts, Christ is their primary delight. Their satisfaction does not solely arise from having material possessions, larger estates, more friends, or greater comforts than others. Instead, their joy comes from knowing how to find Christ in all these things. They see these blessings as a fruit of the covenant that God has established with them in Christ and as gifts flowing from the fountain of God's eternal love and mercy in His Son. In Zechariah 9:11, God declares, "As for thee also, by the blood of thy covenant, I have sent forth thy prisoners out of the pit wherein is no water." This reference to the deliverance of prisoners can be applied to all the mercies that a believer experiences. Every deliverance from evil and every good they possess comes through the blood of the covenant. A believer can look at every meal they have and all the blessings they enjoy and see them as flowing to them through the blood of Christ, making them all the sweeter. It's like the sun's warmth, which is not as intense when it shines through the air alone compared to when it passes through a burning-glass. When sunlight is concentrated through a burning-glass, it becomes more powerful, even to the point of causing a fire. Similarly, the goodness of God that comes to people through His general bounty and patience lacks the power to warm and inflame their hearts and draw them closer to God. But Christ is like the burning-glass held between God and the soul, and when God's mercy passes through this burning-glass, it warms and enlivens outward comforts. Consequently, there is no one in the world who can enjoy worldly comforts with as much contentment as the people of God, for all their blessings come through Christ. Christ is everything to them in the enjoyment of all things. And I could go on to explain how He will continue to be everything to us in Heaven for all eternity.

Now, let me share one more aspect: just as He is everything to us in the blessings we receive from God, He is also everything in everything we offer back to God, in our descent from God to us and in our ascent from us to God. Christ must be central in our offerings, no matter how good they may be. Even when our offerings are spiritual, they must find acceptance with the Father through Christ. This point is emphasized in 1 Peter 2:5: "Ye also, as lively stones, are built up a spiritual house, an holy priesthood, to offer up spiritual sacrifices acceptable to God by Jesus Christ." Take note of "to offer up spiritual sacrifices." Although the sacrifices are spiritual, that alone is insufficient for acceptance; Christ must also be involved. Therefore, the verse adds, "acceptable to God by Jesus Christ." Many people may offer sacrifices and believe that is enough, but the people of God do not rest merely in the duty or even in the spirituality of the duty, although spirituality is considered significant. They take one step further, and this is what you must do in all your offerings to God. Not only should you ensure that your offerings are spiritual, but you must also present them to God in the hands of Jesus Christ and anticipate acceptance through Him. When you approach God in all your acts of worship, make sure not to neglect the work of faith by laying hold of Christ and bringing Him along with you; otherwise, your service will not be accepted. We know that in the Old Testament sacrifices, although they were good, were not accepted unless brought to the priest, and the priest had to offer the sacrifice for them to be accepted. This was a foreshadowing of Christ's priestly role. Christ's priestly work involves taking all the sacrifices we present to the Father and offering them on our behalf, for we must not presume to offer them ourselves. Even if we offer a sacrifice that is excellent, it will not be accepted unless it is offered on the right altar, which is Christ Himself. In all that we offer to God, whether in worship or service, we must look toward the Temple, toward Christ, for He is everything in ensuring the acceptance of our offerings.

And thus, we have concluded with the fourth particular, demonstrating where Christ is all in all.

However, one might ask, why does God choose this method of revealing Himself to humanity rather than the way we might think, relying on the light of nature and reason? It's true, we are sinners, but God is merciful, and we will seek and cry out to Him for forgiveness, mercy, and deliverance from our sins. Why wouldn't God save us in this way? I won't engage in a debate about the feasibility of this approach, but we know that this is not the chosen path.

Therefore, we must now inquire into why God prefers this unconventional path over any other. In truth, when we consider it properly, it is a remarkable path. There is nothing in the world that more deeply affects a person's heart, inspiring adoration and awe for God within the mystery of the Gospel, than understanding that God has a unique method of revealing Himself to humanity, distinct from Angels and all other creatures. This method involves the second person in the Trinity taking on human nature, suffering, dying, and being the sole channel through which we receive God's mercy. This is an extraordinary mystery of godliness and should occupy our serious contemplation.

Now, if you desire to know the reason behind it, firstly, it is so that God can demonstrate to all human beings the immense chasm their sins have created between God and them. We can hardly fathom a way to illustrate this divide more clearly than by this means. When we comprehend that, by nature, we were in such a condition and had strayed so far from God that there was no means of receiving any good from Him except through this extraordinary and wondrous method of a mediator between God and humanity—someone who would obey, suffer, and die for us—we must realise that there was indeed a profound distinction between God and us. Man's state was profoundly low, and his condition was exceedingly dire, requiring such an extraordinary remedy. God wants humanity to comprehend the extent of the breach between Him and their souls, a breach that few truly understand. Even if I were to expound the law to you with all its curses and present the torments of hell before you, none of this could convey the dreadful nature of the breach between you and God as effectively as this point, which reveals that the breach necessitated such a strange and wondrous means for God to be reconciled and appeased towards you.

Secondly, God has chosen this path because He sees it as the most advantageous means to manifest His glory, particularly the glory of His mercy. There is no way, devised by humans or angels, to portray God's mercy in the salvation of mankind more effectively than through this method. If God had simply said to humanity, "You have sinned against me, but I am merciful and will forgive you," that would have been glorious. However, infinitely more mercy is displayed when God declares, "You wretched creatures have sinned against me, and your condition is so dire that unless the Son of my bosom becomes a curse for you, there can be no mercy for you. I am willing to offer Him up, not sparing Him, but giving Him as a curse to prepare mercy for you." This is a truly glorious act. Therefore, when Christ was born, the angels sang, "Glory to God in the highest" (Luke 2:14). It was as if they were saying, "This is the pinnacle of God's glory, to provide such a way of reconciliation with the children of humanity." God was so committed to the task of showing mercy to humanity that He was willing to endure His Son's death. This demonstrates the depth of His infinite mercy and love when it overcomes such significant obstacles. This is the glory of His mercy.

And secondly, there is the glory of His justice: God reveals the glory of His justice more in this way of reconciling man to Himself than if all mankind had been eternally condemned. God's justice would not have been honoured as much in that scenario as it is in His way of reconciling man. This is for two reasons: Firstly, because in Christ, God's justice is actively glorified, whereas if all men had eternally perished, it would have been glorified passively. To have it actively glorified is more significant than passively. Just as God takes more pleasure in active obedience than in passive obedience, He takes more pleasure in the active glory of His justice than in the passive aspect (though there is a sense of activeness in suffering, as seen in Christ's suffering; therefore, the distinction between active and passive is unnecessary, for His active obedience was passive, and His passive obedience had an element of activeness in it).

Secondly, God's justice is now perfectly glorified; the debt is fully paid. If all mankind had been damned, the debt would have been in the process of being paid, but it would never have been fully paid for all eternity. It's like when a poor man owes a thousand pounds and pays two pence a week; he may be making payments, but he can never pay off the entire debt in his lifetime. However, if a wealthy man were to come and pay the full amount at once on his behalf, the debt would then be fully paid. This is much more significant than it perpetually being paid off. So, I say, if all mankind had been eternally damned, God would have had the debt in the process of being paid, but it would never have been completely paid. But now, Christ comes and makes the payment in full, placing it before Justice, asking whether it is satisfied. Therefore, Justice is more glorified in this way.

Thirdly, the infinite glory of His wisdom is displayed in reconciling Justice and Mercy together—God being infinitely merciful and just simultaneously. This is something that no angel in heaven could ever have imagined. Suppose God had said to all the angels in heaven, "Mankind is in a lost and hopeless condition, yet I am willing to save them in a way that reconciles infinite mercy and justice." If they had all consulted together, they could not possibly have conceived how this could be accomplished. Only the infinite wisdom of God, and nothing else, could have devised such a method where God could be both infinitely merciful and just at the same time.

Fourthly, the infiniteness of God's holiness is made manifest through this. If God had simply shown His mercy throughout the world without further action, His holiness and abhorrence of sin would not have been as evident as it is now when nothing but the death of His Son can expiate sin. If God were to take any of you to the brink of hell and allow you to witness the torments of the damned and hear their cries under the fruits of divine wrath, you would exclaim, "How God hates sin!" Yet, be aware that in the sufferings of Christ, there is a greater demonstration of God's abhorrence of sin than in all the torments of hell. To truly understand how infinitely hateful sin is to God, come and witness Christ, both God and man, suffering under the wrath of His Father. Look upon Him in the garden, sweating drops of blood; follow Him to the Cross and hear His cry in the bitterness of His soul: "My God, my God, why have you forsaken me?" Behold Jesus Christ, God-man, who was God blessed forever, made a curse for sin and for your sin. In this reflection, you can see God's hatred of sin. There are two mirrors in which we see the evil of sin: the bright crystal mirror of the law and the red mirror of Christ's suffering. The latter more fully and sensibly reveals the nature of sin and God's hatred of it. By this, you can understand 2 Corinthians 3:18, where the Apostle, speaking of the mystery of the Gospel, says, "But we all, with open face, beholding as in a glass the glory of the Lord, etc." We see only God's back parts in His works, as God said to Moses; we see only the footprints of God in His works. But when we behold Him in Christ, we see Him with an open face. Consider the difference between knowing a man when you only see the imprint of his foot in the sand and when you look him in the face. That is the difference between knowing God and His glory as displayed in the works of creation and as displayed in the face of Christ. To manifest His glory, God chose not to pardon sin as freely as saying, "You have sinned, but I will have compassion on you and forgive you, and that's the end." No, even though He would pardon sin, He would do it in this manner.

A third reason why God would bring about things in this manner is that God foresaw no other way to draw poor sinners to Himself as effectively as this. When God reveals to a sinner that He is not only merciful but has also provided such a unique way to convey His mercy, it has a powerful effect in drawing the soul to God. The poor soul, realizing its own guiltiness and God's hatred of sin, also understands that God's heart is set on this way of mercy. This acts as a compelling argument for the soul to draw near to God in dependence upon Him. The soul may reason, "If God, in His infinite wisdom, has provided such an extraordinary way of conveying mercy to sinners, and He has revealed to me the mystery of the Gospel and His desire to show mercy in this way, then the Lord is willing to be reconciled to me. Why should I remain unbelieving? Why should I have doubts about God? You cannot desire your soul's salvation more than God desires to magnify His grace and mercy, and God has done more for you than you can possibly do for your own salvation. Furthermore, this is a compelling argument because it removes the infinite distance that conscience apprehended between God and the soul. When the soul recognizes that Christ is the mediator between God and itself, this distance no longer appears daunting. Even all your guilt, filthiness, and pollution, as well as the accusations of the law, need not discourage you when you see that you have access to God through Jesus Christ. Therefore, no soul can stand back and say, 'How do I know this applies to me?' Just remember this one rule: nothing can bring the soul to Christ except Christ Himself. There is no preparation for Christ; Christ must be everything in it. So, do not puzzle yourself about your preparations. Instead, present to your soul the mystery of the Gospel in this glorious way of God's self-communication to you and the reconciliation of man to Himself. The very efficacy of these truths will have a profound impact on your heart, drawing you to God in this path of reconciliation, which is the path of true comfort.

The Gospel itself, even without any prior preparation, has the power to draw the heart to Christ because Christ is everything in it. Do not say, 'I am a poor, insignificant creature; I can do nothing. I cannot remember a sermon, I cannot pray, or perform any good duty as I should.' Well, remember, soul, that Christ is everything. It is true that if something were required of you in the matter of salvation, it might be somewhat concerning your weakness. However, understand that God has placed help upon One who is mighty. Therefore, it is not your weakness or the distance between God and you that can hinder you if you rightly apprehend God in Christ reconciling the world to Himself.

Another reason for this could be that God does it to eternally endear His mercy to His saints. Nothing endears God's mercy to them as much as seeing it coming to them through such a unique method of conveyance. What will endear God's mercy to the saints in heaven for all eternity will not be so much the blessings they receive but the extraordinary and wonderful way through which they receive them. This, I say, will occupy the hearts and be a significant part of the glorified saints' work in heaven for all eternity: admiring, adoring, and praising God in Jesus Christ.

And then God delights to honour his Son, and to exalt Him, He makes Him the means of conveying all good to those whom He intends it for. It's as if a king were to honour his son; what better way could he choose than to decree that all the favour he intends to bestow on anyone should come solely through his son? In the same way, when God the Father desires to honour His Son, He decrees from all eternity that all the grace and mercy anyone will receive from Him will only come through His Son. Therefore, just as Christ says, "All judgment is committed to the Son, that all men might honour the Son as they honour the Father," I can say about God's work and dispensation of grace that everything is conveyed to Christ, and through Him, it is communicated to those who have an interest in Him, so that the Son may be honoured for all eternity.

I will conclude with a few words of application to impress upon you what has been said.

First, if it is so, let us pause for a moment and marvel at the depths of God's counsel and the infinite glory of the riches of His grace towards mankind. That God should ever have such thoughts towards such insignificant creatures as we are, and that He chose not to let such despicable creatures perish eternally but to show mercy to them in such a unique way - truly, brethren, God has accomplished more in bringing a poor soul to Himself than in creating heaven and earth. The work of creating heaven and earth is but a lesser feat when compared to this extraordinary way of conveying His grace and mercy to the children of men through His Son. This is the masterpiece of God's works, whether already done or to be done for all eternity. God deserves to be admired and adored for this. We should glorify God in every created thing, but how much more should we sanctify His name when we behold His glory in His humblest works? If it is a sin not to sanctify the name of God when we witness His glory in His most modest works, then how great a sin is it not to sanctify the name of God when we contemplate the mystery of the Gospel and His glory shining in the face of Jesus Christ! God expects (brethren) that those living under the Gospel should dedicate their days, thoughts, and conversations to the contemplation of the glory He has revealed in His Son. For those of you with frivolous and worldly spirits who can squander your precious thoughts on such trivial matters, know that there is an object worthy of your thoughts. Your sin is even greater when you waste your thoughts on vanities while God presents to you such a glorious object to engage your hearts. Those of you who have more time and greater wealth than others, and are not as occupied with the necessities of life, but have greater opportunities for the worship and service of God, and for delving into His truth - how do you squander your time on frivolous and trivial matters, as if there were no greater issues to engage your hearts! It is a sign of a vain and frivolous spirit that, when God presents such glorious things to you, you are content to fritter away your time on vanity and matters that will not profit you. If you want evidence for your souls that Christ is everything to you and will be for all eternity, take it from this: if God has ever opened your eyes to behold His glory in the mystery of the Gospel, and your heart has been captivated and overwhelmed by it, then it is proof that you are indeed the soul whom God has received in His mercy through His Christ. But, as the Apostle says, "If our Gospel is hidden, it is hidden to those who are lost." Many hear the Gospel, yet it remains hidden to them. It is hidden to you if you merely speak of Christ in a formal manner, thinking it sufficient to say, "I hope to be saved by God in Jesus Christ." But do you see in the Gospel that which fills your heart with wonder, eclipsing all the glory of the world? Do you perceive more of God's glory shining in that one sentence, "God so loved the world that He gave His only begotten Son, that whoever believes in Him should not perish but have everlasting life," than you do in the entire creation of heaven and earth? You may hope to get to heaven, but what would you do there? The work of saints and angels in heaven, when joined together, is to magnify God for this great work of His. So begin this work here and give God the glory for the great things He has done for the children of men.

The second use should have been this: If Christ is thus all in all, then let us thank God that we ever knew Christ and that the mystery of the Gospel has been revealed to us. Without this grace of God in the Gospel being revealed to us, we would have been without God in the world. What would have become of us if this grace of God in the Gospel had not been revealed to us? Could you have ever thought of it yourselves? Could it ever have entered into your hearts? Certainly not, nor into the heart of any creature in heaven or earth. Therefore, blessed are your ears that hear the things which you hear, and blessed are your eyes that see the things which you see. Know that when you come to live under the ministry of the Gospel, you enjoy the greatest mercy that you have had since your birth. Coming under a powerful ministry that reveals Christ and brings the day of salvation to the soul is nothing other than the fruit of Jesus Christ's prayer for that soul. Compare Isaiah 49:8 with 2 Corinthians 6:1-2, and you will see this. Isaiah 49:8 says, "Thus saith the Lord, in an acceptable time have I heard thee, and in a day of salvation have I helped thee, etc." It is apparent from the context that this refers to Christ, and God the Father is speaking to His Son. Well, what is this acceptable time and day of salvation in which Christ is heard? Look at 2 Corinthians 6:1-2. In the previous chapter, Paul had told them that they were ambassadors for Christ. He says, "We then, as workers together with God, beseech you also that ye receive not the grace of God in vain." Now, what is this grace of God? It is the ministry of the Gospel. For He saith, "I have heard thee in a time accepted." And note how he applies it, "Behold now is the accepted time; behold now is the day of salvation." It's as if he were saying: "The acceptable time and day of salvation in which God the Father has heard Christ is now, when we, the ambassadors of Christ, come and open the mystery of the Gospel to you. Now is the time in which God the Father hears the Son for you." What a mercy is this, and what an obligation it places upon you! When you hear anything of the mystery of the Gospel opened to you, consider it as the result of Jesus Christ's prayer, and when God sends a faithful minister to any congregation, it is the fruit of Christ's prayer. Christ prays, "O Father, let there be an acceptable time for such a people, for such a man and woman." Perhaps they have long lived in ignorance and profaneness, but Christ has been praying to the Father for them. When this acceptable time comes, then God arranges it so that this person will leave such a wicked family and live in a godly family or come to such a sermon where they will hear the wonderful things of the Gospel explained. They will come to understand this great mystery of God revealing Himself through Christ to His people, and the Lord will renew them by a work of grace, turning their hearts towards Him. This is the acceptable time when God reveals the mystery of the Gospel to any soul. Therefore, bless God for this.

Thirdly, this shows how precious Jesus Christ should be to us. Oh, how should we delight in Him, the One who brings the treasuries of grace from the Father's bosom and opens them to us! He not only reveals the Father's mind to us but also pours out the riches of God's goodness upon us. It was stopped before, but Christ, as it were, opened the floodgates and let the stream of grace and mercy flow upon us. How dear, then, should Christ be to us! It was the testimony of that martyr, Master Lambert: "None but Christ, none but Christ." Yes, when he suffered martyrdom for Christ, then none but Christ was dear to him because he saw that Christ was the means of conveying all good to him. If God now makes a man a means of conveying much good to a nation, everyone will be ready to look up to that man. But there has never been such a means of conveying good to us as Christ. So, how should our hearts love Him, treasure Him, and rejoice at the very thought of Him! If you have a friend, and God makes that friend an instrument of mercy to you, how much more endeared are you to that friend! If a husband is an instrument of good to his wife, or a wife to her husband, or a minister to his congregation, and vice versa in all relationships. When we see others as instruments of conveying God's mercy to us, it is a powerful reason to bind our hearts to them. Indeed, this is the way to gain love. Perhaps a wife complains that she lacks love from her husband, or a husband complains that he lacks love from his wife. Well, be as instrumental as you can in conveying the goodness of God to them, and this will greatly endear and unite them to you. And if this is true among humans, how much more should it be true between us and Christ, who is indeed the husband of His Church and through whom the fullness of God flows to His people! How precious and dear, then, should He be to us!

Fourthly, is Christ all in all? Then, if we have an interest in Him, it should satisfy and content us, even if we have nothing or are nothing in ourselves. Why? Because if we have Christ, we have everything. Though you may lack abilities, friends, wealth, and outward comforts, know that Christ should be your all. Isn't He enough? As He said, "Am I not better to you than ten sons?" So says Christ to the soul, "What do you lack? You may want this comfort and that comfort, but am I not all in all to you, and better than all? Be willing even to be made nothing, for everything is fulfilled in Christ."

Furthermore, it should motivate us to be willing to surrender everything we have to Christ. Our all is but a meager all, yet give it to Christ—our abilities, wealth, interests, and reputations. Let Christ have everything because He is our all.

Let Him be the standard by which we value all things. As much as you see of Christ in anything, value it accordingly. It is said of Master Bucer that if he could discern anything of Christ in a person, no matter how poor or lowly they were, his heart would embrace them. Likewise, it is reported of Augustine that before his conversion, he took great pleasure in reading Cicero's works. However, he later remarked, "I find not the name Christ in all Cicero," and that turned his heart away from such pursuits. So, in everything you enjoy, consider how much of Christ you see in it. Let your delight and esteem be directed toward it to the extent that you perceive Christ in it, and no further.

Moreover, with what fervent intent should the heart be directed towards Jesus Christ above all else! What if God bestows upon you wealth and honour in the world? Without Christ, you have nothing, nothing that paves the way for you to eternity. Therefore, do not be content with anything without Christ. As Abraham said, "What will You give me, Lord, since I am childless?" You should likewise say, "Lord, You have given me a portion in the world, You have granted me honour and respect among people. But Lord, what is all of this to me if I lack Christ and do not have Him, who is the channel of grace to my soul, who is all in all? O Lord, You have taught me today that there is such a divide and breach between You and me that unless it is reconciled through a mediator, I shall perish eternally. Therefore, give me Christ, whatever else You deny me. Do not be satisfied with anything without Christ. Many hypocrites are content with gifts; if they possess gifts, they are content. Consider the parable in the Gospel of Matthew 13:45-46. The merchant sought after beautiful pearls, but when he found the pearl of great price, he went and sold all he had and bought it. Now, gifts, talents, and other accomplishments are those beautiful pearls. But Christ, He is the pearl of great price. Therefore, be willing to part with everything for Him. If God has revealed to you the pearl of great price, do not let beautiful pearls satisfy you. Many souls perish eternally because they are content with beautiful pearls and do not strive to obtain this pearl of great price.

Again, the application should further have been to encourage you to strive to internalize this truth: when seeking God, always bring Christ with you.

I will share only this observation: If it were your final opportunity to pray to God, and your eternal destiny hinged on God's mercy, even if you earnestly sought God, yet if it were solely in a natural manner, as your creator, your situation would be exceedingly dreadful, and you would face eternal damnation. If God were to place any of you on your sickbeds or deathbeds, and you cried out to God for mercy, "Lord, have mercy," make sure you bring Christ with you and view God through Christ, or else all your pleas will be in vain. As Luther once remarked, God looked upon without Christ is most fearsome and terrifying. It reveals great ignorance on our part when we assume that we can approach God and find mercy without acknowledging Him as the God who reconciles with us only through His Son. In conclusion, just as Christ said, "If I am lifted up, I will draw all people to Me," this is the essence of our ministry's work. We have spent time among you with the intention of exalting Christ to you. Oh, may God be pleased to draw all your souls to Him.

This sermon was preached on March 28, 1641.

The Glorious Enjoyment of Heavenly Things by Faith.

Now faith is the substance of things hoped for, the evidence of things not seen. Hebrews 11:1

In the latter part of the previous chapter, the Apostle exhorts to perseverance and highlights the great evil and danger of turning away. To prevent this evil, he explains what will save us from it. Regardless of what others do or the temptations and trials we may face that could lead us astray, the righteous shall always live by faith. Now, faith is the substance of things hoped for, the evidence of things not seen.

In this chapter, he explores the topic of faith, providing an excellent description (though not an exact definition) of it. It is the substance of things hoped for, the evidence of things not seen. The term "substance" used in the original text is rich in meaning, signifying the fundamental nature, the foundation of the things hoped for. It is the subsistence, the substantiality of those things that do not presently exist for us but are future and the object of our hope. Faith grants them a real, substantial existence for us, even though they are yet to come. The substance of things hoped for, the evidence of things not seen. The word "evidence" carries a logical connotation, denoting a type of conviction that results from dispute and clear demonstration, compelling one to accept it. This word's propriety lies in the fact that although the objects of faith are unseen, either by the senses or reason, faith provides such illumination and clarity that it forcibly leads the soul to believe in them. Thus, faith offers the most complete possible conviction.

So, two key aspects of faith are highlighted here:

First, it imparts a substantial, real, and present existence to the things hoped for.

Second, it serves as the evidence for things not seen. In the first aspect, we recognize two key points: first, that the Saints have many glorious things they hope for, even though they do not possess them—they are people of hope. Second, their faith imbues these hoped-for things with a genuine and substantial existence.

In the second of these, we also find two key points: Firstly, that the things of God are unseen. Secondly, that faith serves as the evidence for those unseen things.

Regarding the first point, briefly, the Saints hold great hopes for things they have not yet received; they are people of hope. They hope that they will soon be delivered from all sin and sorrows, never sin again, never be tempted again, never suffer again, and never fear again. They hope for a time when all their sins will be like the Egyptians, as Moses said, seen no more. They hope that their lowly, sinful bodies will soon become glorious bodies, shining more brilliantly than the sun in the sky. They hope that the Image of God will be perfected in them, uniting them fully with God, just as the Father and the Son are one. They hope to meet their blessed Savior in the air, with their own eyes beholding Him in His glory. They hope to possess the glorious mansions He has gone ahead to prepare for them. They hope to gaze upon the deity and see God in a manner that transforms them into His likeness. They hope for complete communion with the Lord, experiencing the immediate and uninterrupted outpouring of deity into their souls and bodies. They hope to join the blessed Angels and Saints in eternal Hallelujahs, perpetually admiring and adoring the name of the great God for the glorious mysteries of redemption through Christ. They hope to keep an eternal Sabbath, free from the concerns of the natural world, and to enjoy perfect and everlasting rest in Christ, living in God as if in an infinite ocean of excellence. These are the things they hope for. But are these mere fantasies, notions, or pretty fancies that bring them pleasure? Is there any substance in these hopes? If these hopes were as real and substantial as the things they currently enjoy in the world, and if they could see them as certainly as they see the things before their eyes, it might be something. However, the Apostle states that there is a principle that can make all these things substantial to you, and that is faith—it is the substance of things hoped for. These hopes are not mere ideas and notions but are kindled in their hearts by the mighty power of the Holy Ghost. Romans 15:13 confirms this: "Now the God of hope fill you with all joy and peace in believing, that you may abound in hope through the power of the Holy Ghost." The power of the Holy Ghost is not required to create fanciful ideas in people's hearts, but the hopes of the Saints are generated within them by the power of the Holy Ghost. God Himself is associated with their hopes; He is called the God of hope. God is not the God of fantasies and ideas but is the God of the hopes of His Saints. These hopes are given to them to prevent them from turning back and to sustain them through whatever suffering they may endure. Therefore, Scripture likens our hope to an anchor and a helmet. Of all dangers, shipwreck at sea and encountering enemies on land are the greatest. Our hope serves to protect against both dangers: against the perils at sea, our hope is an anchor, and against the perils on land from enemies, our hope is a helmet.

The hope of the Saints, for the present, is like the cork to the net, keeping it from sinking to the bottom. Even when they are in the water and weighed down by the lead of troubles and afflictions, their hope keeps them afloat. They possess great hopes, and these hopes are made substantial by their faith, for their faith is the substance of the things they hope for. Now, let's consider the second point: Carnal hearts believe that true excellence lies only in the outward aspects of the world. They assume that money, lands, honours, and the pleasures and delights of the flesh possess real substance and are truly substantial. They view these things as having genuine value. However, I beseech you to observe the disparity between the judgement of the Holy Ghost and that of a carnal heart. While a carnal heart regards outward things as the only substantial ones (hence why you call rich individuals "substantial" people), the Holy Ghost deems those things that the world perceives as substances to be mere illusions. On the other hand, the Holy Ghost considers things that the world regards as illusions to be substantial. Those who judge according to the Holy Ghost share this perspective. To illustrate the first point, consider that St. John classifies all things in the world into three categories: profits, pleasures, and honours. He calls them the lusts of the flesh, the pride of life, and the delights of the eye. Now, for the things that the world regards as its greatest substance, such as wealth and riches, take note of how the Holy Ghost views them. Proverbs 23:4-5 advises, "Labour not to be rich: cease from thine own wisdom: wilt thou set thine eyes upon that which is not?" In other words, what you consider your substance, the Holy Ghost says, does not exist at all. Now, you might argue that honours and promotions have some substance in them, but the Holy Ghost disagrees. Acts 25:23 recounts how Agrippa and Bernice arrived at the judgment seat with great pomp, wearing splendid clothing. However, the word translated as "great pomp" could also mean "great fancy." What greater honour is there for princes than to arrive in their robes at the judgment seat, glittering before the eyes of their subjects? And yet, according to the Holy Ghost's judgement, their great glory was nothing more than a grand illusion. As for the pleasures of the flesh, Amos 6:5-6 vividly describes the sensuality of the people: they lie on beds of ivory, stretch out on their couches, consume the choicest meats and drink wine from bowls, among other indulgences. In verse 13, it all boils down to this: "Ye rejoice in a thing of naught, in that which hath nothing in it." There is no genuine substance or substantial excellence in any of these things, be it riches, honours, or pleasures. Now, let's examine how the Holy Ghost judges spiritual matters: it finds substance in them, while carnal hearts consider them mere illusions. In Proverbs 8:20-21, Wisdom claims, "I lead in the way of righteousness... that I may cause those that love me to inherit substance." In this context, substance means true existence. Hebrews 10:33-34 offers further insight: "You were made a gazing stock both by reproaches and afflictions, and took joyfully the spoiling of your goods, knowing in yourselves that ye have in heaven a better, and an enduring substance." So, the things that were mere illusions to the world became substantial to the believers through their faith. In Hebrews 11:10, Abraham is said to have looked for a City with foundations. In Abraham's eyes, no city in the world had foundations, except for the one he hoped for. It was his faith that provided foundations for that City. Thus, we see the contrasting perspectives of the Holy Ghost and the world. While we live on Earth, we perceive the Earth as vast and the Sun, Moon, and Stars as relatively small. However, were we in heaven, we would view the Sun, Moon, and Stars as immense bodies, while the Earth would seem insignificant in comparison—a mere point. Likewise, when individuals possess worldly hearts, they perceive heavenly things as illusions, trivial, and unworthy of pursuit. But if they were elevated to heaven by divine principles, they would recognise the greatness of heavenly things and view earthly matters as insignificant and unworthy of attention or attachment. The objects of faith are substantial, and faith imparts that substance to them.

And they are substantial things, firstly, because they contain more than initially meets the eye. We consider something substantial when it possesses more than it outwardly presents. Those things that make a grand display but lack the depth of substance are deemed vain and insubstantial. For instance, if a piece of cloth does not match its appearance, lacking the qualities it seems to possess, we say it lacks substance.

Now, the things of God contain far more within them than they outwardly reveal, and therefore they are substantial. When Christ comes in glory, the text says, "He shall be admired in all them that believe" (2 Thessalonians 1:10). Believers currently perceive a significant level of excellence in Christ, loving Him for what they currently see. However, when Christ appears in the future, His glory will far surpass their expectations. They will say, "Indeed, we did see much in Christ, but now we behold infinitely greater glory and excellence than we ever imagined."

Secondly, heavenly things, the objects of faith, are substantial because they contain the essence of God within them. God is the infinite first being of all, the source of existence for everything. Therefore, what possesses the most of God's essential being within it must be the most substantial and genuine good. While it is true that all creatures reflect God's excellences, spiritual and heavenly things are filled with God to a greater extent than any other. They contain God's divine nature, His life, His image, His glory, and it is where God communicates Himself most fully. God communicates in two primary ways: one is to His Son in an incomprehensible manner, and the other is to His creatures. The special communication of Himself to His creatures is found in spiritual and heavenly matters. Therefore, they are unquestionably the most substantial and real things to the soul.

Thirdly, they are substantial things, not mere notions or conceits, because they are at the very core of God's thoughts and intentions. They represent what God aims for in all His works with His creatures and constitute the pinnacle of happiness for the most excellent creatures He has ever made. Something that results from God's grand design for the world and all His works, and that represents the highest good a creature can attain, must undeniably possess substantial existence. The goodness found in spiritual and heavenly things is the ultimate outcome of God's eternal purpose, in His complete communication of Himself to His creature, and it is the highest good any creature can achieve. Therefore, spiritual things are real and substantial.

Furthermore, they are real and substantial because they produce a genuine and substantial effect on the souls of those who are acquainted with them. The apprehension of spiritual things, the objects of faith, has a profound impact on the hearts of the godly. Spiritual things have the power to uplift and elevate the hearts of individuals who were previously lowly, base, impure, and unworthy, enabling them to engage with God in the highest possible manner. They empower the soul to accomplish great deeds. Such substantial effects can only result from real and substantial things.

Lastly, they possess an eternal existence that will never fade or diminish. While all other things may wither like the grass, spiritual and heavenly things will endure forever. Hence, they are the only substantial things.

Now, how do they become substantial to the soul? It is through faith; faith provides them with a firm foundation and substance of being. I emphasize this because the primary reason why our hearts are not captivated by spiritual things is that we fail to perceive their reality and substantial nature, as well as the immediacy of the goodness they offer.

Faith grants them this substantial existence:

Firstly, faith leads the soul to contemplate God Himself, enabling it to recognize the excellency and glory inherent in God, to comprehend aspects of God's essence and existence. It elevates the soul to engage with

God in a manner far surpassing the capabilities of reason alone, although reason indeed provides some understanding of God. Moreover, faith allows the soul to discern the riches found within these excellent and glorious aspects of God. It initially perceives them in God and subsequently acknowledges that God is infinitely willing to share and reveal Himself to His creatures. Furthermore, faith enables the soul to engage with the profound and glorious purposes of God, established between God and His Son. It discerns the grand design God had in sending His Son into the world to fulfill the lofty and glorious intentions of communicating Himself to humanity through a mediator. Additionally, faith considers the profound depths of the covenant of grace, discovering the immeasurable riches hidden within—riches that reason or the created world cannot fathom. One of the primary objects of faith is the covenant of grace in the Gospel, where it perceives the revealed riches. Faith also receives the testimony of the Holy Spirit, appointed by the Father and the Son to bear witness to these grand truths, revealing to the soul the deep mysteries of God. While these matters may be mere notions to a person's heart without the Spirit of God, the Spirit of God unveils them to the soul. Thus, when faith engages with these objects and embraces them as its rightful sphere of operation, it transforms all the glorious truths concerning the eternal happiness intended for those chosen by God into substantial and tangible realities for the soul. These are truths upon which the soul can confidently build and risk its eternal destiny. When venturing one's eternal condition, a strong foundation is crucial. Since it is the task of faith, when God intends to save the soul, to possess such convictions of the Gospel that it is willing to stake its eternal state upon it, it must be built upon a solid foundation. Consequently, faith is the substance of things hoped for and imparts a genuine existence to these things.

Furthermore, faith not only makes these things real and substantial but also imparts another aspect to them—presentness. Although they are things hoped for, faith grants them an immediate existence in the soul. By faith, they are perceived as currently existing, even if they do not possess such existence in themselves. Faith shares similarities with the nature of God, as it possesses a sort of omnipotent power to create something out of nothing. There are numerous remarkable works of faith, and among them is a significant one—providing present substantiality to that which lacks it, making it a genuine and substantial reality to the soul. This particular function of faith is quite noteworthy. It can distance itself from impending evils that are very near and encompassing, as seen in Psalm 91:7: "A thousand shall fall at thy side, and ten thousand at thy right hand, but it shall not come nigh thee." It is a peculiar expression to claim that it shall not come nigh thee when thousands fall on both sides and one is in the midst of them. Faith is responsible for this achievement; it places at a distance what is right upon you. When a deadly plague is a considerable distance away, reason can offer some sense of safety, as one might think, "I am safe enough because it is far away." However, if the plague were to enter your house or chamber, believing in a promise that it shall not come nigh thee represents a mighty work of faith. Faith creates a gap between present and approaching evils.

On the contrary, for absent good things that are situated far away, faith has the power to make them appear as if they genuinely exist. Hebrews 11:13 mentions the Fathers, who saw the promises afar off and embraced them. The word used in the original text is "saluted" the promises. When friends salute each other, they must be in close proximity. Their faith made promises that were distant seem as if they were present. Therefore, Abraham saw Christ's day and rejoiced. The Scriptures also discuss taking hold of eternal life, accomplished through faith, and receiving the end of your faith. Psalm 108:7-8 says, "God hath spoken in his holiness, I will rejoice, I will divide Shechem &c. Gilead is mine, Manasseh is mine." Notice the phrase "is mine." The immediate conclusion is as if the matter were already accomplished, for it was so through faith. Faith provides a current existence to things. Reason itself has considerable influence in making future events appear as if they were present, both for harmful and beneficial matters. In the case of evil, a contemplative individual with a wicked heart can draw the sweetness of a distant lust and sin closer by meditating on it and repeatedly thinking about it. Such a person can engage in sinful contemplation even though they might end up in hell before actualizing it. Just as reason and discourse can draw in a lust and make it appear as if it were present, it can also do the same for future positive events. This distinction underscores the difference between rational and sensual creatures. A sensual creature is interested only in what is immediately before it, whereas reason can bring in distant matters and make them seem as if they were present. In this regard, God has a significant advantage over humanity, whether for bringing His wrath upon them or bestowing happiness upon them. Just as you can bring your lusts that are absent and make them seem present by using reason and contemplation, God can make future evils and plagues appear present to you through this faculty. Consequently, the dreadful fate of those who perish eternally can be described in a horrifying manner: they are rational creatures who, by using reason, can bring all the misery they will endure for eternity into the present moment, experiencing every moment of that eternal misery immediately. Conversely, those who are saved will experience boundless happiness in every moment because they can bring all the happiness they will experience for eternity into each present moment. This is the function of reason. If reason can make future events appear present, how much more can faith, which is not just elevated reason but a principle higher than reason? Despair, for example, brings hell upon a person before they are actually in hell, making the future torment a real existence in the heart as if it were present. Some individuals in their despair have cried out that they are in hell, feeling the flames of hell upon them. Despair brings the reality of God's future wrath close and immediate. In the same vein, faith brings the reality of

God's love and mercy that is yet to come and makes it present. It is a genuine work of faith to make future things present, akin to any other work of faith. While I should have explained in what ways faith makes future things present and what the work of faith entails in them, I will provide a brief summary. Faith makes all things that are yet to come present.

Firstly, faith sees all things as certain, as if they were already a reality. For instance, if a person holds a bond worth one hundred pounds that they are sure of, they consider it as a hundred pounds in hand due to its certainty.

Secondly, faith perceives the possession of things, not just that they will be acquired in the future, but that there is a present possession of them. This happens in two ways. Firstly, Christ, our leader, has gone ahead to prepare mansions for us and has taken possession of heaven in our name. Therefore, we have taken possession in Him. Secondly, we have received the first fruits of the Spirit, the initial blessings of the glorious things of heaven. In this respect, we have taken possession ourselves, which is why they appear as present to faith.

Thirdly, eternity is so vast that the time before we have full possession is insignificant, so faith regards them as present.

Fourthly, faith continually keeps the things of heaven in view, and they are thus present because they are always in the sight of faith.

Fifthly, their presentness is evident because the Saints experience everything in God. The happiness of heaven lies in seeing all glory and blessedness in God. Faith enables us to glimpse some of this here. Enjoying communion with God presently, beholding heaven in God, and seeing all things in Him must necessarily make them exist presently and truly in the soul.

So, I have briefly discussed how faith serves as the substance of things hoped for.

In terms of practical application, if faith is the substance of things hoped for and grants reality to such lofty and divine things, then faith itself must be an exceedingly substantial thing. It is not a mere concept or notion, as it gives reality and substance to what the world deems as mere notions. Faith is one of the most substantial and glorious elements in the world. It is through faith that the power of God is most evidently displayed, as seen in Ephesians 1:19-20, where several levels of God's extraordinary power are revealed in the workings of faith. This underscores that faith possesses a remarkable essence. Indeed, faith encompasses much, for even though it is a grace that humbles us, it empowers believers to perform one of the most magnificent acts a creature can undertake. To have a soul acknowledge its own wretchedness, burdened by sin and guilt, and recognize the wrath of an infinite deity directed towards it, along with the infinite justice of God demanding satisfaction and His infinite holiness abhorring sin. Confronted by the accusations of conscience, Satan, and the world, and fully aware of these afflictions, yet choosing to lay hold of a mediator between God and humanity, placing trust in a righteousness beyond oneself, offering it to God the Father as complete atonement and satisfaction, and daring to stake one's eternal destiny on it. Despite its inherent impurity and filth, faith enables one to unite with God in a bond as close as possible, given the nature of the relationship, almost akin to the hypostatic union between the human nature of Christ and the divine. Undoubtedly, faith accomplishes a profoundly noble and glorious work, demonstrating the abundance of God's power within it.

In light of this, we can discern the emptiness of the faith held by the majority of people in the world. Their faith is devoid of substance; it is mere emptiness, merely a notion. It is no wonder, then, that everything they believe remains as mere notions, and their faith remains ineffectual. You claim to hope, believe, and trust in God's mercy, but what practical and substantial impact does your faith have on your hearts?

When genuine faith enters, it brings with it the mighty power of God and His wondrous glory into the soul, almost as if it creates and bestows real existence upon the loftiest and most glorious objects in the world. Therefore, recognize that faith is not a lifeless, shallow entity in the soul; it exerts a powerful influence on the hearts of both men and women. Certainly, the faith that can save a soul must exhibit lofty and glorious effects within the soul.

Furthermore, if faith imparts substantial existence to things hoped for, then we must learn to strengthen and exercise our faith in the objects of our hope. Which one of us does not aspire to attain great and glorious things (as I previously hinted at)? Therefore, let faith be actively exercised and fortified in these matters. If all these blessed things we spoke of were present in the soul, how elevated our hearts would be above worldly matters! We would regard all earthly things as insignificant and worthless. Our thoughts would be captivated by the wonder of spiritual and heavenly things, our spirits would be kindled with love for God, and our conduct would reflect heavenly priorities at present. We would harbor heavenly thoughts and heavenly affections in all our ways, and we would willingly face any trial, endure any hardship, and sacrifice anything for God. If our faith could make such glorious things as these genuinely substantial to us, then our duties and services would also possess true substance. Why is it, then, that our duties often seem so futile and empty, devoid of anything but outward form? Certainly, brethren, if our faith can give a substantial reality to the blessed and glorious aspects of eternal life, it can equally bestow substantial reality upon all our duties and services, ensuring that we do not present empty and lifeless offerings to God. Therefore, do not content yourselves with a faith that fails to grant substance to your duties, and do not expect it to grant substance to the magnificent things we have spoken of. This concludes the discussion of the first point: "Faith is the substance of things hoped for." Now, I would like to touch briefly on the second point: "It is the evidence of things not seen."

This involves two aspects:

Firstly, that matters of grace, spiritual and heavenly in nature, are not visible.

Secondly, that faith provides evidence for these matters.

Firstly, it is essential to understand that grace, spiritual things, and heavenly blessings are not seen.

The Apostle states in Galatians 5:19-22 that the works of the flesh are evident. However, when he addresses the works of the spirit, he does not claim that they are evident, for indeed, they are things that are not visible. Although the effects of these works may be apparent, there is no external manifestation of grace that distinguishes them, and even a hypocrite can mimic them. Thus, the works of the spirit cannot be considered visible, either to the senses or to reason. Concerning heavenly matters, the Apostle says in 2 Corinthians 4:18, "While we look not at the things which are seen, but at the things which are not seen, for the things which are seen are temporal, but the things which are not seen are eternal." I had intended to elucidate why spiritual and heavenly things are not seen by presenting many arguments, but I shall now select a few key points. The spiritual and heavenly treasures of a Christian are analogous to the riches of the sea. On the surface, one may only observe turbulent waves and a great deal of impurity, yet the true riches lie beneath. Similarly, the riches and treasures of a Christian are not visible; they are concealed within the very heart of God. Just as no one knows the thoughts of a man except the spirit of man, no one knows the thoughts of God except the Spirit of God and those to whom God has revealed them.

Furthermore, these things are beyond the scope of reason; they are too exalted and too magnificent for a faculty like reason to comprehend. Just as an object too brilliant for the eyesight can blind it, these objects are too exalted for reason and therefore cannot be seen by it.

Additionally, human blindness, which is inherent, prevents individuals from seeing these things. Chiefly, God arranges events in His providence in a manner that seemingly contradicts His promises, making it contrary to the perceptions of the senses and reason. God often hides His mercy towards His own people in this manner. Consider the case of Abraham, to whom God made two promises: first, that He would lead him out of his homeland to a land flowing with milk and honey, and second, that He would make his descendants as numerous as the stars in the sky, and through his seed, all the nations of the earth would be blessed. When Abraham arrived in Canaan, the promised land, he faced a famine and had to flee to Egypt for sustenance. Additionally, Sarah, his wife, was barren, and it seemed impossible for her to bear children. Despite receiving a child, Abraham was tested when he was asked to sacrifice Isaac, the son of promise, and although Isaac survived, he did not marry for another forty years, and even then, he did not bear children for twenty years. Over the course of 150 years, there were only seventy descendants of Abraham, yet the promise was that all the nations of the earth would be blessed through his seed. God appeared to be acting contrary to His promise. Similar instances can be found in Jacob's life. God commanded Jacob to return from Laban, but on his journey, Laban pursued him with intentions to harm him. During his journey, his wife's nurse and wife died, his daughter Dinah was raped, and his sons Simeon and Levi committed a terrible act that caused Jacob's reputation to suffer. Finally, his brother Esau approached with hostile intent. All of these adversities occurred during a journey that God had commanded Jacob to undertake. If Jacob had not possessed faith, enabling him to see beyond these challenges to the unseen promises, it would have been impossible for him to persevere. When God led the Israelites to Canaan, they embarked on a lengthy journey through the wilderness. Upon their arrival, they encountered the harshest region of the land, the arid and barren south, seemingly contradicting the promise of a land flowing with milk and honey. God's providence appeared to be at odds with His promise, obscuring the excellence of His blessings and making them invisible. In light of this, it becomes clear that the things of God are not perceptible to a carnal eye and require more than reason alone to apprehend them.

Firstly, we should cease to be surprised that individuals with exceptional intellect and reasoning abilities do not perceive the things of God but disregard them. Do not be troubled by this; these are unseen things. Many are deceived into thinking that because certain individuals possess greater intellectual capacities to comprehend natural phenomena, it necessarily follows that they have deeper insights into spiritual matters. They reason thus: "Why do you simple men and women understand these things when there are great scholars and learned individuals who do not?" This line of thinking reveals a carnal disposition, as if the strength of human reason could enable individuals to comprehend more than faith can achieve. You may recall Christ's words in Matthew 11:25: "I thank you, Father, Lord of heaven and earth, that you have hidden these things from the wise and understanding and revealed them to little children." Nevertheless, the mindset of worldly individuals is evident; they often regard religion as foolish and absurd. This extends to religious fervor as well; when one observes another deeply committed to something they consider inconsequential, they cannot help but deem it foolishness. Therefore, when worldly individuals witness God's people passionately engaged with things they find devoid of excellence, and see them willing to risk and endure for these beliefs, they regard it as folly and madness.

Just as Pontius Pilate reacted with skepticism when Christ spoke of truth in the face of a life-threatening situation, so too do carnal individuals dismiss the actions of God's servants who are willing to sacrifice their wealth and lives for what they perceive as insignificant matters. This dismissal arises because the things of God are unseen. Consequently, in

matters of spiritual and heavenly significance, we must consistently strive
to diminish the role of reason and elevate that of faith. As Martin Luther
stated, "In matters of God, we must not constantly seek reason, for these
are unseen things." Luther also emphasised that faith "slays the beast of
reason" in spiritual matters. While reason does serve a purpose when
controlled by faith, it should be viewed as a beast that must be subdued
to allow for a clearer perception of spiritual matters.

I have come across a story in a book about a gathering of bishops, during which a philosopher engaged in a dispute against the Christian faith
and presented such subtle arguments that left the bishops perplexed.
However, a godly yet humble man among them requested permission
to speak, despite their initial concerns about his perceived weakness.
They eventually allowed him to speak, and he presented certain religious principles to the philosopher, simply asking, "Do you believe these
things?" He repeated this question several times, and as a result, the
philosopher capitulated. He remarked that he had heard nothing but
words until then, but now he felt a divine power working within him,
and he could no longer resist the Christian faith. This transformation
occurred solely through the presentation of the objects of faith and the
persistent inquiry, "Do you believe?" Indeed, in matters of faith, belief
often precedes full comprehension. Sometimes, our faith must aid our
understanding rather than the other way around, as demonstrated in the
case of Peter in John 6:69. Peter declared, "And we believe and are sure
that thou art the Christ, the Son of the living God." Notice that he said,
"We believe and are sure," not "We are sure and believe." Belief comes
first, and certainty follows; by believing, we attain assurance. Many individuals desire to be certain that Christ died for them, that their sins
are forgiven, and that they are God's children. They attempt to establish
this certainty through various arguments and by examining the effects,
seeking to identify specific indicators. However, the Apostle's approach
here should be our primary one: "We believe and are sure." We should

commit our souls to the truth of God's word and, through belief, attain certainty.

So much for the first point: the things of God are things not seen.

Now, as for faith, it provides evidence and clarity. As stated in 2 Timothy 1:12, "We know in whom we have believed," and the mercies of God in Christ are referred to as "The sure mercies of David" in Acts 13:34. Faith is not a mere notion, imagination, or conceit; rather, it is what makes everything sure and certain for the soul. I should address a question here: Can there be faith without assurance, that is, without assurance of one's own salvation through Christ?

Certainly, it would be a significant error to equate faith with the riches of faith, which is assurance. The Scriptures refer to assurance as the riches of faith. Just as a person can conduct their trade without being rich, so too can one be a believer without being rich in assurance. Assurance is the cream of faith, the riches of faith. I should have explained how far faith can serve as evidence, even in the presence of doubt. Only this much: the assurance we gain through faith, by relying on the Word and drawing conclusions from divine principles (which I should have elaborated on — how faith transforms things into evidence through divine and spiritual principles, and what these principles are, but we cannot explore this now), is an evidence to the extent that the soul can confidently rely on it, as I mentioned earlier. Faith is a foundation upon which the soul can confidently venture. As one martyr stated, "Though I cannot argue for the truth, I can die for the truth." When faith arrives with a convincing light, even if doubts, fears, and temptations persist, the soul can trust and depend on it. The soul resolves, "If I perish, I will perish here. Let the whole world say what they will; I have found this to be the way, and regardless of the outcome, I will not turn back." In this way, faith overpowers the soul and carries it through opposition, and thus, faith serves as evidence.

Many things should have been addressed by way of application.

Firstly, if faith is evidence for other things and makes them visible, then it can also serve as evidence for itself. I mean this: it is possible for a soul to know its own good condition and its connection to Christ solely through the work of faith itself. Even if it cannot presently argue a posteriori from the effects of faith, it can argue a priori; faith can provide evidence for itself. Many Christians continue to doubt because they believe they must have evidence of their faith through certain effects that follow their faith, and until then, they can have no comfort. It is true that where true faith exists, there will be fruits and effects of it. However, if you could grasp this Gospel mystery and find evidence within faith itself, you would arrive at comfort more quickly, and it is a much safer approach. When you have doubts about your condition, fear that your sins are not forgiven, and doubt your connection to Christ, the way to overcome these doubts and fears is to renew the act of faith itself. Present to your souls the riches of God's grace in the Lord Jesus and see if it draws your souls to believe. Even if your hearts do not respond immediately, present these things to your souls repeatedly, and do not turn from renewing the acts of faith to dwelling on your corruptions. Instead, look upward repeatedly, and through this process of viewing, a power will arise to draw your heart to believe. Just as the presentation of the law has the power to terrify and frighten, the presentation of the glorious aspects of the Gospel has the power to draw out faith. You must renew the initial act of your faith, to embrace Christ and rely on God's grace in Christ. Even if you find various corruptions within your heart and are tempted to think, "Should someone as polluted and defiled as I am cast myself upon God's grace in Christ?" seize Christ nonetheless. You have as much reason to do so as anything else, and this must be your course: to repeatedly renew this initial act of faith. You may say, "But my doubts and fears persist." If you want evidence, repeat it a thousand times over, and eventually, evidence of the act of faith itself will emerge. You may argue that this could be seen as presumption to cast oneself upon God's free grace in Christ. I reply, this is not presumption because the very act itself grants you a right to everything in God and Christ. Presumption occurs when a person takes something they have no right to, but if an action grants them a right, it is not presumption. You might argue that this is a licentious way and allows for liberty. Do not misjudge faith. When you, even in the absence of sight and sense and without reason for doing so, venture yourself upon God's grace in Christ, it is the most glorious work you can perform in this world. Even if you were able to overcome all your corruptions and perform the greatest imaginable service, it would not be as glorious as this. It is also the most difficult thing in the world; therefore, it is not a doctrine of liberty. A soul that can overcome all the difficulties of faith, conquer its boundless guilt and the terrors of the law, and venture upon God's free grace in Christ despite all obstacles, can overcome any difficulty in the world. Many other things could have been mentioned to reinforce this point. Even when we are in the dark and cannot see, sight and sense are absent, and exercise faith. If you wish to magnify God as a Christian, this is the only way. There is a remarkable example of trust that Alexander placed in his physician, and the trust he bestowed upon him greatly honored him before all his nobles. When Alexander fell ill, someone warned him to be cautious of his physician, claiming that someone had bribed him to poison Alexander. The physician brought him a potion, and Alexander handed him the letter. He immediately drank the potion, indicating that he did not believe the accusations against his physician. This action greatly honored the physician. Likewise, when you have no evidence in yourself, and even when faced with many temptations that cast doubt on God's grace in Christ, temptations that suggest Christ has abandoned you and things would not be this way if Christ intended good for you, even when temptations are at their most intense and speak the worst of Christ — at that very moment, to venture your soul upon Christ, Christ will regard it as the greatest honor you are capable of bestowing upon

Him. It is also the most effective way to enhance the riches of His grace and mercy. Be cautious of unbelief as well as presumption. Fear that you may fail to magnify the riches of God's grace in Christ, which is His primary purpose among humankind. I had intended to provide some encouragement for believing in cases where there is a lack of evidence, when we are in the dark and cannot see any light. I also planned to offer guidelines to aid our faith.

But I will conclude with this one use.

By what has been delivered, you may all see what an excellent and admirable grace faith is and how useful it is. Oh, brethren, in these times when there is such fear, trouble, and distraction, having faith to give substance to all the things that God has spoken of, to give substance to all the glorious promises that God has made to His people, what a wonderful blessing this is! Now exercise your faith and, by faith, give substance to all these promises; make them a foundation to rest upon. Be willing to risk everything you have—your estates, names, liberties, lives—for the furthering and fulfilling of the glorious promises that God has made to His Church. If you have faith that gives foundations to those promises, you will do so. Even though we see nothing but darkness and misery in the world, let us exercise faith. If the hour of temptation is yet to come, as who knows, then we shall need faith, and only faith can help us find light in such darkness. To prepare for such times, labor to strengthen your faith, and from what you have heard, you can see how valuable faith will be in any danger. It is a great comfort to a Christian that, although he is in the dark about many things (such as the disputed truths about churches and the like), he knows he has something within him that will make the things of eternal life evident to him. It is a wonderful blessing from God to have a principle that gives substance and evidence to such things. Many poor souls would greatly rejoice if they could have evidence of just one truth of religion, like the truth of a deity, which reason sheds light upon. They are so plagued by atheism that they would give a thousand worlds to be rid of it. Now, if having evidence for one principle of religion is such a great mercy, what a glorious mercy it is to have faith that provides evidence for all the glorious things of God and makes them clear and plain to you! You can remember a time when you thought of them as fantasies and notions, but now you see them as clearly as the light of the sun, and you wouldn't trade that sight for a thousand worlds. In the future, brethren, when we see these things not through faith but through our senses, oh, how we will bless God then that we had evidence for these things in our souls! What would have become of us if we hadn't had evidence to make these things clear to us, to reveal the righteousness of God in Christ for eternal life? I saw these things existing and evident before, and now God fully reveals them to me. On the other hand, those who lack a principle of faith to make these things substantial and evident to them, when these things become substantial and evident to their senses, what a dreadful terror it will be for them! Then they will say, "Oh Lord, if only I had seen these things before, my heart wouldn't have been so captivated by the things of the world. I pursued the vanities of the world, seeking riches and honors, thinking I was the only happy person, and considering those things the only substantial and real things. The things I heard the preacher speak of, I thought were mere notions and conceits. But now I see they are real and substantial. Oh, miserable person that I am!"

Oh, the work of faith that can enable those with weaker understanding to perceive the great things of God, as stated in James 2:5. "Listen, my brethren," says the Apostle, "God has chosen the poor of this world to be rich in faith." To comprehend the profound and glorious aspects of faith; that poor individuals should grasp the great, deep, and hidden things of God, which have been concealed since the beginning of time, is a remarkable achievement. Therefore, when John inquired of Christ whether he was the Messiah, Christ provided this as one argument: "The poor receive the Gospel," as mentioned in Matthew 11:5. But was this an argument in favour of Christ being the Messiah, or was it an argument against him because only the poor received it? If the great and influential had embraced it, that would have been an argument. However, "The poor receive the Gospel." It is a testament to the mighty power of God that those who are poor and weak in worldly matters can have this powerful work done in their souls, enabling them to receive Christ and the Gospel.

Brethren, having the use of our physical eyes, which allows us to behold the great works of God, such as the Sun, Moon, and Stars, and to recognise the glory of God in them, is a great blessing. What person would be willing to lose their eyesight in exchange for the entire world, given that it reveals so much of God's glory? Now, if the eye, which can only perceive these natural phenomena, is so precious, then what can be said of the eye of faith? It may rightly be called precious faith, for it admits into the soul the glory of God, the excellences of Christ, and the great things of eternal life. These are brought into the soul by faith, in their reality and power, to elevate the heart, fill it with joy and peace in believing, and carry the soul through all the trials of this world. Oh, the eye of faith is a precious eye! The eye of the senses is precious because it enables us to see tangible objects, but the eye of reason is even more precious because it can make visible things that are not seen by the senses. Reason can reason its way up to God Himself. It is the incredible excellence of a rational being that God has endowed with the ability to reason from effect to cause and from one cause to another until ultimately arriving at God, the first cause of all. This is a remarkable gift for which we should thank God. But now, if the use of reason is so excellent because it provides evidence of rational things, then we should strive to hold this precious faith in even higher esteem. This faith provides us with evidence of the glorious things of God, the faith that God has placed in our hearts for the very purpose of enabling us to receive those glorious and hidden mysteries of godliness that are of infinite importance to our eternal well-being.

This sermon was preached on April 25, 1641.

The Natural Man's Bondage to the Law, and the Christians' Liberty by the Gospel.

"If the Son therefore shall make you free, ye shall be free indeed." - John 8:36

I n this chapter, we find Christ continuing His dispute with the argumentative and peevish Jews, responding to everything they say, even though they criticize nearly every word He utters. However, while the crowd's response was mixed, some were captivated by His words. In verse 30, it is mentioned, "As he spoke these words, many believed in him," or at least there were early signs of faith or some readiness for it.

Christ goes on to tell them in verse 31 that to be His true disciples, they must continue in His teachings. It's not enough to be moved in the moment and claim belief; Christ expects them to persist in His word. How often do convictions that briefly touch people's hearts and consciences fade away, leaving nothing behind? They fail to continue in the word of Christ and, therefore, are not truly His disciples.

Furthermore, Christ tells them that they need to understand more about their spiritual condition than they currently do. "And you will know the truth, and the truth will set you free" (verse 32). He seems to say that although they may have some vague perceptions of things at present, their understanding of their condition is limited. If they continue on the path God has started by convicting their consciences, they will come to know more than they presently do. "You will know the truth, and the truth will set you free."

But in verse 33, they respond by saying, "We are Abraham's descendants and have never been enslaved to anyone. How can you say, 'You will become free?'" Here, they begin to dispute again. John Calvin suggests that these words may be from other Jews present, not those previously mentioned as believers. However, some argue that even those who began to believe might have said this because, despite their initial assent to Christ's teachings and significant conviction, there was still a great deal of stubbornness and crookedness in their hearts. They resumed arguing with Christ, especially when He hinted at their spiritual bondage.

It's common for many people, including those who experience convictions of conscience and the initial work of God's Spirit in them—perhaps even saving work—to remain stubborn and resistant for a long time, especially when faced with opposition. Thus, they retort, "Are you speaking to us about bondage and freedom? We've never been enslaved by anyone" (verse 33). "Never in bondage to anyone?" Were not the Jews in captivity to the Babylonians at one point? And were they not currently under Roman rule? Nevertheless, they assert, "We were never in bondage." Carnal hearts, until fully transformed by grace, often resist acknowledging their wretched state. They are averse to hearing anything that reveals the misery they are in. "We were never in bondage," they claim. Despite their resistance, Christ pities them. He doesn't immediately withdraw because He sees their persisting stubbornness and their objections to what He is saying. Instead, He clarifies the type of bondage He is referring to. In essence, He says, "The truth is, even though you consider yourselves free, there is a form of bondage you are in—a bondage that only the Son of God can set you free from. If the Son, therefore, makes you free, you will be truly liberated." Thus, we arrive at the words of the text.

These words, you see then, present to us the blessed liberty of the Gospel; the freedom that believers enjoy through Christ.

I now proceed to the central doctrinal conclusion, which is this:

There exists a blessed liberty that Christians experience through Christ alone. This doctrine of Christian liberty enjoyed through Christ is a treasure trove of abundant comfort, and much of the Gospel's mystery is encapsulated within it. To attempt an exhaustive discourse on this doctrine, delving into all its aspects, would lead to excessive length and an attempt to grasp too much. If we were to intend a comprehensive treatment, I would need to show you: 1. What Christ sets believers free from. 2. The privileges of this freedom bestowed by Christ. 3. The recipients of this freedom – who possesses it. 4. Its bestowal – how it comes through the Son, exclusively through Him. 5. The price and acquisition of this freedom. 6. The claim that believers have on this freedom – how they become enfranchised and acquire a share in it. 7. The application of this freedom. But should I proceed in this manner, I would be able to achieve little. Therefore, I won't attempt to encompass so much. My intention is to address just one specific aspect of our freedom through Christ.

If I were to first explain what we are liberated from, it would entail freedom from the law, freedom from the dominion of sin, freedom from the bondage of fear, freedom from a condemning conscience, freedom from servility in the performance of holy duties; we are emancipated even in our holy duties; freedom from death and its evil, and freedom from the devil's tyranny, along with freedom from the ceremonial law. However, we mustn't attempt to encompass all these specifics. To illustrate our freedom in these areas, I shall focus solely on one, namely, our freedom from the law. "If the Son, therefore, shall make you free, you shall be truly liberated."

The doctrine of freedom from the law is the topic we shall explore today. When I speak of freedom from the law, I do not mean freedom from obedience to the law. It is an erroneous notion to believe that we are freed from obedience to the law. Moreover, it is an idea so base and absurd that it is not worth our time, especially given the little time we have and the profound importance of our subject. For what is the law but the image of God, the very reflection of God's wisdom and holiness? If one regards it as requiring obedience, then for anyone to claim we should be freed from obedience to the law is tantamount to saying we should be freed from the image of God, from the reflection of God's wisdom and holiness. Therefore, we will not spend any time on this notion. When I speak of freedom from the law, I mean liberation from the law's severity and from the condemning verdict of the law, in which all its severity is manifest.

Consequently, it is necessary to first provide you with an understanding of the bondage we all find ourselves in under the law, unless delivered by Christ.

And then, secondly, I shall endeavour to elucidate wherein the liberty of the Gospel lies, which Christ has acquired for us. These two aspects, brethren, constitute the core of theological doctrine, and unless you are well-informed and grounded in these two aspects, you will not have a correct understanding of any religious point.

Regarding the first aspect, I will be concise, even though it encompasses many particulars, for my primary focus is on the second aspect. As a prelude to this first aspect, I must inform you that I will mention many things that may appear exceedingly challenging. However, bear in mind that, although these things may seem difficult, they serve the purpose of preparing you for what I will subsequently impart, which will bring much comfort and peace. If I speak of your bondage, it is solely to help you appreciate the blessedness of your freedom and liberty.

Therefore, to comprehend what you are liberated from, namely, the rigour of the law, you must understand what this entails and what all of you are subjected to by nature when considered apart from Christ. For the Holy Spirit expresses our subjection to the law; He says we are under it (Romans 6:14). There was a time when they were under the law. Firstly, the rigour of the law is manifest in that it demands difficult things from those under its authority. I will explain later how these demands are not so to those set free by Christ. However, to those under the law, it is a harsh yoke. It requires challenging tasks that go against the inclinations and dispositions of all under its jurisdiction, tasks that provoke enmity and antipathy in their hearts. To demand actions that are contrary to one's nature and elicit aversion from one's nature is very burdensome. Yet, all the duties of the law fall into this category for those in bondage to it.

Secondly, the law requires not only difficult but impossible tasks, tasks that cannot be accomplished by those under its dominion. The law is a yoke that neither we nor our forefathers could bear (Acts 15:10). You might argue that this pertains only to the ceremonial law. While that is partially true, there is more to it. Consider the context of this statement. It arose because some individuals from the Church of Jerusalem went to the Church of Antioch and troubled the disciples with two doctrines: the necessity of the ceremonial law and justification by the law. The comment about the yoke is directed at both. It was not only the ceremonial law through which they sought justification, but also the moral law, and both were yokes that neither they nor their forefathers could bear. It must refer to both because in the very next verse, it is contrasted with the grace of Christ (verse 11). It conveys that you should not anticipate salvation through the law but through the grace of the Lord Jesus Christ. The grace of the Lord Jesus Christ opposes not only justification by the ceremonial law but also justification through obedience to the moral law. Hence, the moral law is a yoke that neither we nor our forefathers could bear. It demands the impossible from those under its sway. We must not presently debate how this can be or its justice; that discussion will follow later.

And then, thirdly, the law demands perfection from all of us. The law accepts nothing less than absolute and complete perfection in every way, including the principle from which it stems, the manner in which it is followed, the rule by which it is governed, and the end to which it leads. It demands absolute perfection.

Fourthly, the law demands that the work must be carried out in our own persons. It is akin to a strict creditor who insists on receiving full payment, down to the last penny, directly from us. In essence, the law demands a flawless righteousness from our own beings, or else it condemns us. This is the righteousness of the law, as stated in Romans 10:5: "That he that doth the things therein contained, shall live by them." It requires personal action – one must perform the deeds themselves or not at all.

However, it might be argued that although much is demanded, some remission might be granted based on one's efforts.

In the fifth place, the law is so rigid and unforgiving that even if we make every effort to obey it, all our endeavours are in vain if they do not measure up to perfect obedience. Many people erroneously claim that they do what they can, have good intentions, and make genuine efforts. While this may hold true for those who are children and enjoy freedom through Christ (as you will hear shortly), those under the law find that their endeavours to obey, no matter how earnest, are not accepted by God if the work is left incomplete.

Sixthly, the law demands unwavering constancy in all aspects. Suppose we could obey the law in everything or make significant progress in many areas. Still, the terms between God and us, as long as we remain under the law, are such that even if we were capable of obeying the law in all respects throughout our lives until the very last moment, and should then fail in any one particular, were it not for the freedom granted to us by this Son, we would be eternally lost. As you progress, you will continue to recognise the immense importance of our freedom through Christ. You must take heed of how you attain deliverance through Christ, for this is undoubtedly your condition as long as you are under the law.

Seventhly, the law exacts obedience with extreme severity, demanding it forcibly from all who are under its jurisdiction. It approaches them with a harshness similar to Pharaoh's taskmasters. The law insists on the work, without considering one's strength – whether one has the strength or not, the work is demanded, and it is demanded with utmost severity, accompanied by dreadful threats if it is not fulfilled. This is why the law was delivered in such a fearsome manner, with thunder, lightning, earthquakes, and fire, to the extent that it caused even Moses to tremble at its delivery. In Deuteronomy 33:2, it is described as a fiery law, delivered with great rigour. This constitutes the seventh point.

Eighthly, there is also this severity in the law: upon the slightest breach of it, it utterly disables the soul from ever performing obedience to it again. The covenant of the Law is so unforgiving that it can be likened to an iron or brazen wall. When a breach occurs, the soul is like an earthen vessel that shatters against it and is broken into pieces. It requires a creating power to make the soul whole again. Please consider, I beseech you, that this is the nature of the Covenant of Works, established in Adam, which has now become the covenant of the Law. Upon any breach, the severity of the law breaks the soul to the point where it is utterly unable to keep it again. It uproots all the principles that would enable the soul to obey once more. Sins against the Gospel do not have this effect, as you will hear later. This is the very reason why, upon Adam's first sin, we all fell, and the Angels did the same upon their sin, as they were dealing with God only in a covenant of works. But if, upon a breach of the Law, all the principles enabling us to keep it are eradicated, it will (we hope) show us mercy and not demand obedience from us.

Therefore, in the ninth place, despite this, the Law continues in its curse and demands perfect obedience, with the threat of eternal death for any transgression, as if we still possessed all the principles necessary to obey it. This is the severity of the Law; it does not relent in its threats, punishments, or the strictness of obedience, even though we have lost all ability to obey it.

Furthermore, in the tenth place, it demands this of us and provides us with no strength whatsoever to fulfill its demands. It finds us devoid of the principles we once had for obedience and offers no new principles. Some have compared its severity to Pharaoh's taskmasters: it demands the production of bricks but provides no strength.

Moreover, in the eleventh place, in all that it does, it threatens our very lives. The Law is not satisfied with mere affliction; if it is transgressed even in the slightest degree, all the afflictions in the world will not satisfy it. Its severity is such that it threatens life, both temporal and eternal. It relentlessly pursues us, leading to temporal and eternal death. I could further explore the condemning sentence of the Law, but that would require a separate discussion. Thus, I only mention here that the Law threatens our lives with every transgression.

Again, twelfthly, its severity is evident in that upon any breach, it immediately binds the soul (even if it does not execute the punishment immediately) with the strongest bonds possible, leading to eternal death. It may suspend the execution, but the bond is immediately sealed upon the breach. Consequently, upon every breach of the Law, all individuals have chains placed upon their souls. These chains represent the guilt of sin, binding them to eternal death with bonds that all the power in heaven and earth combined cannot release.

Thirteenthly, next, the severity of the law is such that once it is offended, it can never be appeased by anything we are capable of doing. Suppose we have offended the Law in some way, even just once; if we then strive with all our might to obey the Law and make up for the breach we have caused, we can never fully satisfy it again. It is true that some, though offended, may find favor again through increased diligence, but with God, under the law, once it has been broken, all the care and diligence in the world cannot make amends; and that is a significant aspect of the law's severity.

However, what can we do but mourn, cry, and rend our hearts because of this distressed condition we are in?

Fourteenthly, the Law does not accept repentance; it will not absolve the guilt of any sin, no matter how much sorrow is expressed. This is a common misconception among people. When they have sinned, they believe they can make amends by being careful, mourning, and repenting, etc. While this holds some value if you are under the covenant of grace, if you are in your natural state, no amount of weeping, mourning, or crying for even one sin, even a sin of thought, throughout your entire life will be accepted unless you come under the blessed liberty purchased by Christ. Therefore, it is crucial to understand the distinction between being under the Law and under the Gospel.

Fifteenthly, furthermore, the severity of the Law is such that once it has revealed our wounds and miseries, it offers no means of deliverance. It is like a surgeon who opens a wound but does not apply a remedy. Were it not for a Mediator, we would find that the Law only exposes our wounds and then leaves us in despair.

Sixteenthly, on the other hand, our bondage to the Law is such that instead of mortifying our sins, it actually stirs them up and makes them worse. While it does threaten severe consequences for transgressors, it does not mortify any sin. Inadvertently, it tends to stir up our sinful desires and exacerbates our sins.

Seventeenthly, there is one more aspect to consider. Even if we were to keep the Law, its promises are modest and pale in comparison to the promises of the Gospel. I am not saying that the promises of the Law are entirely temporal, although prior to the revelation of the Gospel, there were few spiritual promises. We know what the Apostle says in 2 Timothy 1:10, that life and immortality have been brought to light through the Gospel. While I do not claim there are none, there are very few Old Testament Scriptures that speak of eternal life.

Now that you understand your bondage under the Law, you will surely appreciate the blessed condition of being freed from it. It is one sign that a soul has been delivered from the bondage of the Law when it can hear all of this and acknowledge God's justice in it, with the heart lifted up to God upon hearing it. However, if a soul, upon hearing these things, deems them to be so difficult and unreasonable that it is inclined to rebel against them, it is a sign that the spirit is not acquainted with them. Although these things may seem challenging to us, if we consider just a few specific points, they will not appear as insurmountable.

Firstly, consider that you have to deal with a God of infinite justice and worth. If we were to regard God as we do a creature like ourselves, we might find it exceedingly difficult. However, when we understand that we are dealing with a God of infinite worth, we should not consider it to be hard.

Secondly, we may not find it difficult to comprehend if we consider the state of perfection in which God originally created man. Regardless of our current condition, God initially provided us with the resources to engage in obedience and fulfill the requirements of the law.

Thirdly, if we truly understood the nature of sin, we would not be surprised that upon committing sin, we find ourselves in the woeful condition we speak of. If we view sin as an attack on an infinite deity, a direct assault on the very essence of God Himself, then it becomes less astonishing that one sin could lead to such a challenging situation.

Fourthly, if we contemplate things that we typically accept but are equally challenging, they may not appear as difficult. For example, the fact that God cast the Angels into eternal torments for a single thought without any negotiations for peace, or that God condemned all of mankind for one sin in Adam, both of which are commonly accepted in general terms. Furthermore, the idea that God the Father treated His beloved Son in such a way, making Him a curse for humanity and subjecting Him to the weight of His wrath, causing Him to sweat drops of blood and cry out, "My God, my God, why hast thou forsaken me?" If you had never heard of such occurrences, they might seem as difficult as anything we have discussed.

Now, before we proceed to address the other aspects, let what has been mentioned thus far help us recognize that all individuals in their natural state face a challenging situation. Just as the Israelites, when their bondage under Pharaoh increased, saw themselves in an evil condition, I implore you to learn to recognize your own state outside of Christ. Understand that you are in an evil condition, in a sad and perilous situation when you hear these things.

Secondly, if it is the case that every soul is naturally in such bondage to the law, then the salvation of a soul is an immense and extraordinary undertaking. It is a task so great that God must mobilize heaven and earth to save a soul and free it from the bondage of sin. The reason people tend to underestimate this tremendous work of salvation and mediation through Christ is because they fail to recognize their bondage. When you truly grasp the nature of this bondage, what it means to be under the law (so far, I have not addressed the condemnation or the curse of the law, but solely the bondage imposed by the strictness of the law), you will understand that saving a soul is an enormous undertaking.

Thirdly, this reveals the futility of the empty arguments put forth by carnal hearts. What can you now rely on—your good intentions, desires, and resolutions? You may lament and grieve because you feel you are not better, and you may strive to do your best for God. While these are commendable things, are they what you rely on to stand before God? If they are, it is likely that you do not comprehend the terms upon which you stand before God or the nature of your bondage.

Fourthly, if God reveals Himself to a person solely through the law, that person's soul is inevitably driven away from Him, viewing God and His law as enemies, unless it is revealed alongside the Gospel. Now, I am about to explain that liberty we have through the Gospel.

Therefore, for the liberty of the Gospel, it is a precious freedom in which the treasury of the mystery of grace is stored. It is the sole foundation of support for our souls. Saint Paul, who was a significant instrument of God in expounding the doctrine of Gospel liberty, articulates it in all his Epistles, often with great elegance. In one passage that presents some difficulty, Galatians 4, beginning from verse 21 and onward, he states, "Tell me, ye that desire to be under the law, do ye not hear the law? For it is written that Abraham had two sons, the one by a bondmaid, the other by a free woman. But he who was of the bondwoman was born after the flesh; but he of the free woman was by promise." These things are allegorical; they represent the two covenants: the covenant of works and the covenant of grace. The covenant of works was given at Mount Sinai and leads to bondage, represented by Hagar. "For this Hagar is Mount Sinai in Arabia, and answereth to Jerusalem, which now is, and is in bondage with her children. But Jerusalem which is above, is free, which is the mother of us all. For it is written, rejoice thou barren that bearest not, break forth and cry thou that travailest not: for the desolate hath many more children than she which hath an husband."

The text may appear somewhat obscure upon initial reading, yet it brilliantly elucidates the doctrine I am currently discussing, which concerns bondage under the law and liberty under the Gospel. The allegory is drawn from the two sons Abraham had, one by a bondmaid and the other by a free woman. "It is an allegory," says the Apostle, "and it signifies the two covenants: the covenant of works, that was from Mount Sinai, where the law was revealed, which leads to bondage, represented by Hagar." Luther noted that "Agar" in the Arabian tongue means Mount Sinai, as they call it in the Arabian language. Therefore, the Apostle alludes to this, explaining that the law associated with Hagar leads only to bondage. Hagar's descendants were Gentiles and remained in bondage, without enjoying the privileges of the children of the free woman. Consequently, all those who engage with God under the covenant of works are bondmen and do not partake in the privileges of the children of the free woman, the children of God. "This Agar is Mount Sinai in Arabia and answereth to Jerusalem, which now is, and is in bondage with her children." The Apostle illustrates the condition of the Jewish Church, Jerusalem as it exists at the time, as a state of bondage when compared to the Church of the Gospel, as they had limited knowledge of the Gospel and were in bondage to the law, knowing little else but the law. "But Jerusalem which is above," referring to the state of the Church under the New Testament, "is above" in relation to the Gospel, which is free and the mother of us all. The Church of God under the Gospel is the "Jerusalem which is above." The text further states, "rejoice thou barren that bearest not, break forth and cry thou that travailest not; for the desolate hath many more children than she which hath an husband." In other words, those who embrace the doctrine of Gospel liberty initially appear barren, like the barren woman before her time of fruitfulness. Just as Sarah was initially barren but later bore a child, the doctrine of Gospel liberty may seem barren for a time until people become acquainted with it. Our role as Ministers of the Gospel is to bring forth children to Christ. If we were to preach only the law and adhere to legalism, we would produce children of bondage, akin to those of Hagar. However, our primary responsibility is to beget children of the free woman, to generate children through the free grace of God in Christ. I earnestly wish I could bring even one soul to this freedom. I cannot help but think that there may be many here who are still children of Hagar, who may have experienced terrors and fears in their consciences yet remain in bondage. The Gospel proclaims liberty to those under bondage. Consequently, it is worth noting the time at which the Jubilee Trumpet was to be blown, as specified in Leviticus 25:9, "Then shalt thou cause the Trumpet of the Jubile to sound on the tenth day of the seventh month, in your land." This day of atonement was a time of public repentance and fasting for the sins of the people, a day of self-affliction and prayer. The Jubilee Trumpet was to be blown on this very day, following the people's heartfelt remorse for their sins. Therefore, if anyone here has been humbled before the Lord and afflicted themselves due to sin, behold, the time has come to blow the Jubilee Trumpet to such a soul and proclaim liberty in the name of Christ. As the Psalmist states in Psalm 89:15, "Blessed is the people that know the joyful sound." By some translations, it is rendered as, "Blessed are they that know the joyful sound of the Jubilee." With reference to our Jubilee in Christ, those who hear this joyful sound proclaimed in the Gospel are truly blessed.

Now, the first aspect of this joyful sound of the Jubilee and the liberty proclaimed by Christ from the law is this: you shall not be condemned for your eternal state by the law. The law may terrify you, but it shall not condemn you. It must indeed condemn those who are in bondage to it for their eternal state. However, if you are a believer in Christ, if you are a child of the free woman, this is your liberty. I repeat, you shall not be condemned for your eternal state by the law. We do not prefer to have any crucial matters determined by those who are rigid and severe. Take comfort, O believer, you have heard of the severity of the law, but the crucial matter concerning your soul and eternal state transcends the law. It has nothing to do with you. You often hear dreadful threats from the law, and these threats may often terrify you. You may be inclined to say, "Who can stand before this holy God?" But be at peace, you believing soul, for you have been set free from the law by Christ, and this is the first joyful sound.

The second joyful sound of liberty that you have through the Gospel is this: your lawgiver is none other than He who is your husband. You now have to deal with no one else in matters of your soul but with Him who is your husband and your advocate. Everything is governed by Him. As stated in 1 John 2:1, "If we sin, we have an advocate with the Father." Advocate implies that you now deal with Christ, your lawgiver, who, upon every transgression, immediately becomes your advocate with the Father. He stands up to plead for you and answer all accusations against you. In other words, He undertakes for you and employs all the influence He has with His Father on your behalf. You now have to deal with Him, your lawgiver, concerning your soul and eternal state, and this is the second joyful sound that you hear from the Trumpet of the Jubilee of the Gospel, proclaiming the liberty you have through Christ.

Thirdly, having been delivered from the bondage of the law, this is now your liberty: you are a law to yourself. What I mean by this is that nothing is now required of you that is not written in your own heart. God writes His law on tablets of stone, and everything required of you in obedience to it is written in your heart. Therefore, you no longer yield obedience to the law because of its condemning power and the punishment it entails but rather from a principle of love for it. We must understand that we are not released by Christ from obedience to the law; we are still obligated to obey the law. However, the difference lies in the fact that we are not enslaved to the law; we keep it willingly. You now keep the law by being a law to yourself and by having everything that God requires of you in His law written in your heart by the law of sanctity that He has given you. That is the third joyful sound.

The fourth joyful sound is this: by the liberty you now have through Christ, your condition is such that whatever you do, even if there are numerous imperfections in it, God will take notice of the smallest good thing in you and disregard all the evil. If God detects even a trace of His Spirit in you, He will make note of it. If there is but a speck of gold, even if it is mixed with a multitude of impurities, God will not discard it but will find it. God is not meticulous in observing what is done amiss by His children, but He is meticulous in noting what is done well by them. The law tells us, and even a moral person will affirm, that to make an action good, all circumstances must align. However, the liberty of the Gospel tells us that where there is any good or any grace in an action, God observes and takes note of it. To provide just one example, which is excellent for this purpose, consider 1 Peter 3:6, where the Apostle presents Sarah as a model for virtuous women: "Even as Sarah obeyed Abraham, calling him Lord." She never called him "Lord" except when she did so in unbelief. Yet God takes note of that word and never mentions her unbelief. Now Sarah was a free woman, and this is how God graciously deals with the free woman. If you are a child of the free woman, this is your privilege: God will take note of every good action you perform. Isaiah 42:3 states, "A bruised reed shall he not break, and the smoking flax shall he not quench." The word signifies that as soon as the flax begins to blacken, God will not reject it. Therefore, if there is even the slightest trace of good, it is accepted. That is the fourth joyful sound of the Gospel.

The fifth joyful sound is this: even if you cannot perform any action, God accepts your willingness and desire as if it were the actual deed. Many carnal hearts find comfort in this, but it applies to those who have been set free by Christ. Perhaps you cannot pray, but presenting yourself before God, as the Apostle suggests, will be accepted by God. And rest assured, if there is any excuse to be made for you, Christ will discover it and present it before God on your behalf. This is the fifth joyful sound.

The sixth aspect of the liberty we have through Christ is that, although the Gospel calls for obedience, it does so in such a sweet and loving manner that it would make any heart in the world fall in love with it. It draws people with the cords of love, as stated in 2 Corinthians 5:20: "Now then we are ambassadors for Christ, as though God did beseech you by us." The Gospel pleads with you to be reconciled to God. In Philippians 2:1, it says, "If there be therefore any consolation in Christ, if any comfort of love, if any fellowship of the spirit, if any bowels and mercies, fulfill ye my joy." The Gospel does not come with thunder and lightning like the law on Mount Sinai. Instead, it approaches in a gentle and mild way, alluring and drawing the soul to itself. This is the sixth joyful sound.

The seventh joyful sound of the Gospel is that it arrives gently but also brings abundant life and strength with it. It comes in line with the spirit, and where the spirit is, there is power, as the Apostle mentions. Luther commented on Romans 8, stating that the law is a spiritual law because it is the law of God, but it is not the law of the spirit of life. It is the law of the Gospel that brings the spirit of power and life along with it. There is a virtue accompanying the commands of the Gospel, empowering the soul for obedience. The Gospel bestows grace and strength beyond what Adam possessed in two ways: it grants the power, the will, and the deed.

The eighth joyful sound of the Gospel is the tender pity and compassion of God towards those who have been set free by it. This distinguishes the sins of those under the law from those under the Gospel. The sins of those under the law make them detested by God, while the sins of those under the Gospel make them objects of God's pity.

The ninth joyful sound is this: the Gospel has a powerful ability to soften the heart and lead it into sorrow and mourning, a kind of mourning that is highly pleasing to God. The law, as I mentioned earlier, does not accept repentance, but the Gospel does. The tears of repentance that come from believers, next to the blood of Jesus Christ, are among the most precious things in the world. I repeat, after the drops of the blood of Christ, the tears that flow from your Evangelical repentance are most pleasing to God. This is the ninth joyful sound.

The tenth joyful sound is this: the Gospel comes with healing. It possesses both a melting power and a healing power. Christ is depicted as coming with healing in His wings. While water may intensify the burning of lime, oil, which fuels other things to burn, quenches that burning. Similarly, the oil of the Gospel, for which Christ was anointed, serves to heal you and extinguish your lusts and corruptions. In Isaiah 57:18, we find an excellent promise: "I have seen his ways, and I will heal him."

The eleventh joyful sound is that, having been set free by Christ, even if you sin not only against the law but also against the Gospel, your sins against the Gospel will not have the power to eradicate any habits of grace. The grace of the Gospel will continue to support the habits of grace within your soul. In contrast, the law, with one transgression, not only eradicates the habit that opposes that transgression but all other habits as well. However, the grace of the Gospel preserves the habits of grace within us.

The twelfth joyful sound is this: the Gospel is so full of grace that it takes advantage of our misery. This is a compelling argument consistent with the Gospel's nature. "Pardon my sin, O Lord, for it is great" is a remarkable argument from a child of the free woman. It is God's argument, as seen in Genesis 8:21: "I will not destroy the world again, for the imagination of man's heart is evil from his youth."

Thirteenthly, another joyful sound of the Gospel is that it proclaims this liberty to us: all that is required of us can be done and accepted by and through another, namely Christ.

Fourteenthly, the grace of the Gospel reveals a way in which God can have all the wrongs committed against Him by your sins made right. While the Gospel proclaims that God is willing to pardon, it goes beyond that by providing a way for God to be fully compensated for all the wrongs you've done to Him. The Son who sets you at liberty has undertaken this task and accomplished it.

Fifteenthly, another joyful sound of the Gospel is this: there is a most absolute perfect righteousness made over to us. The righteousness of the Son of God belongs to you; it has been transferred to you to be presented before the Father on your behalf.

Sixteenthly, furthermore, there is this joyful proclamation of the Gospel: it offers remarkable promises, glorious and elevated things, even the infinite treasures of God's grace. The Son has come from the bosom of the Father, revealing the treasures of God's grace and disclosing things that were kept secret since the foundations of the world.

Seventeenthly, and yet there is one more thing necessary for the complete consolation of the liberty of the Gospel, for this blessed Jubilee to truly resonate in your heart. That is, the covenant of the Gospel is so constructed, and Christ has undertaken for you in such a way, that it can never be forfeited. This is the full, rich, and glorious grace of the Gospel: Christ has pledged himself to the Father, and the Father has promised and engaged His own truth, mercy, and faithfulness to ensure that this covenant will never be voided. Even the condition of the covenant that is required of you is that which Christ has undertaken to perform in you before the Father. If perseverance is a spiritual blessing, it is part of Christ's purchase and must stand. Therefore, be at peace, for you are in a condition where you cannot forfeit or break the covenant. The marriage covenant between you and your Savior can never be dissolved.

I should have elaborated more on the blessedness of this liberty, emphasizing that all this grace comes through the Son, not merely from God's general bounty. In a higher way, we gain our liberty through the Son of God, who is both God and man, the heir of all things. Thus, we become co-heirs with Him. However, I must conclude here.

This sermon was preached on April 21, 1641.

A Preparation for Judgment

"But after this the judgment." - Hebrews 9:27

The scope of the Holy Spirit in this Epistle is to prove the excellence of Christ, that He is the Messiah who was to come into the world, and that all the types and shadows of the law pointed to Him. A special part of the Epistle is to show the superiority of Christ's Priesthood over the Priesthood of Aaron. Among other considerations, it is pointed out that the Priests offered sacrifices frequently, whereas Christ offered Himself only once. This one offering of Himself is eternally effective and requires no further offering. The Holy Spirit illustrates this by comparing the efficacy of Christ's sufferings with the efficacy of human actions in this world. Just as the actions of people in this world, whether good or evil, have eternal consequences, and what a person does in this life determines their eternal state, so the death of Christ is eternally efficacious. It is appointed for men to die once, and then comes judgment.

By "judgment" here, I do not believe the Holy Spirit primarily refers to the judgment of the final day (although it is true that after death, the judgment of the final day will follow, and all people must face judgment). However, I will not speak further about the judgment of that day. Instead, I believe the Holy Spirit's intention here is to refer to the individual judgment that occurs immediately after death, which determines the soul's eternal condition, either of happiness or misery.

While people are alive, their eternal condition is not definitively determined by any act of God, even though God's eternal purpose remains unchanged. Even the saints themselves often experience fears and doubts about their eternal state during their earthly lives. They would eagerly seek deliverance from these fears and doubts, as they are burdensome. After death, however, this longing will be fulfilled. This is the benefit that death brings to believers: after death, they will face judgment, meaning they will be securely established in their eternal state, free from all hazards, fears, doubts, and temptations. They will never fear or doubt again about their eternal destiny, nor will they lose any of the blessings they possess. This is the judgment that awaits the saints after death.

On the contrary, wicked men in this world may hold hopes and confidence that everything will be well for them. However, after death, judgment awaits them. This means that when a wicked person dies, their hopes perish. They are irrevocably placed in a condition where they will never have hope of anything good again. They are beyond any hope or possibility of receiving further mercy from God. This is the meaning of the verse on both sides: "But after this the judgment." Regardless of people's conditions in this world, the saints, who may have many fears and doubts about their eternal destiny, will be securely established in eternal happiness immediately after death, free from all doubt. Conversely, despite the hopes and confidence that wicked people may have in this world, all such hopes will vanish immediately after death when judgment comes. Job expresses a similar sentiment in Job 8:14, "The hope of the hypocrite is like the spider's web; he weaves a cunning web out of his own spirit, but the broom of death sweeps it all away in an instant. For immediately after death, judgment awaits."

This, then, is the doctrinal conclusion that we need to discuss based on these explained words:

The only opportunity men have to secure their eternal condition is during their earthly life. If it is not done in this life, there is no help afterwards, because judgment follows after death.

I would like to address this point in a way that can inspire and motivate you to take action during your lifetime to ensure your relationship with God. After death, judgment awaits.

This point that I am about to address is one of the most solemn matters concerning humanity. It is often one of the first things that the Lord impresses upon the hearts and consciences of those He converts to Himself. When a person who has been living in sinful and destructive ways suddenly stops and reflects, asking questions like, "Lord, where am I? What am I doing? What will become of me? Why was I born? Why did I come into this world? What is my purpose here?" God answers by saying, "Your purpose here is to make provisions for eternity. It is about this significant task—to reconcile all matters between you and God. Be diligent in it, for although your life is short and uncertain, this crucial task hinges on the brief and uncertain period of your earthly existence. If it is neglected during this limited time I have given you, you are lost and doomed forever, because judgment follows immediately after death. You will then be placed in a position where there can be no alteration. The Schoolmen have observed that what happened to the Angels who sinned is analogous to what happens to wicked men in death. Just as the Angels were irreversibly condemned upon their first act of sin, so are wicked men when they die. While we live in this world, even in our sinful state, our condition is considered better than that of the fallen Angels. We are not definitively and irreversibly judged in our earthly life. However, once death arrives, a wicked person's condition becomes identical to that of the fallen Angels: irrevocable, certain, and unchangeable. While we preach to people, no matter how wicked and ungodly they may be, we offer grace and mercy in Christ because they have not yet faced the judgment described in the text. But if this offer is repeatedly ignored, and the fragile thread of your life is eventually severed, then you are eternally lost. For judgment swiftly follows after death."

In reflecting on this point, it seems to me that I cannot help but envision God as looking upon all the children of men in their fallen, lost, sinful, and miserable state with pity and compassion. He might say, "Poor creatures, they have sinned against me and have made themselves liable to eternal wrath, which they do not comprehend and cannot bear. Well, I will grant them a little time to seek their pardon and reconcile with me. I will provide them with the means to do so. However, they must take heed, for their eternal destiny will be determined by how they use the time I give them. If they neglect it, they are lost forever, and mercy will be of no avail to them. The way we all hold our lives is like that of a condemned malefactor granted a temporary reprieve by the favor of the Prince. He is given a little time and the possibility of seeking a pardon, and his fate depends on how he spends that time—whether it leads to life or death. Similarly, our lives are held on this uncertain ground. We are all condemned before the Lord, but God, in His infinite grace, has provided a way of salvation for humanity. He grants us a limited time (however long we live, be it two or three days) to make peace with Him. If we neglect this opportunity, all is lost, and we are doomed forever. Great consequences hinge upon this brief, uncertain period of our lives. Alexander the Great was said to set up a burning lamp and proclaim that whoever sought favor and life while the lamp was burning would find it. But those who waited until the lamp went out were condemned to death and could expect no mercy. Brothers and sisters, God has set up a lamp, and that lamp is our life. God proclaims that whoever seeks His mercy while this lamp is burning will find it. But if you wait until the lamp goes out, only eternal misery awaits. Your life's lamp may not only go out when its oil is consumed but also by accidental means. If this lamp is extinguished and your work is unfinished, you are lost forever. Solomon, when preparing the Temple, made everything ready in advance so that there was no noise of axe or hammer heard there. Likewise, those whom God intends as living stones in the glorious Temple of Heaven are shaped and fitted here. There is no room for repentance and sorrow for sin after this life; what needs to be done must be done here. Ecclesiastes 9:10 tells us, "Whatever your hand finds to do, do it with all your might, for there is no work or device or knowledge or wisdom in the grave where you are going." The way you fall when you die is the way you will lie eternally: toward God, and He will be yours forever; or toward sin, and misery and destruction will be yours forever. Ecclesiastes 12:7 states, "Then shall the dust return to the earth as it was, and the spirit shall return unto God who gave it." The souls of wicked men also return to God, the One who gave them, but it is to receive the sentence of their eternal doom and be established in their everlasting condition. There is a profound change in the soul immediately after it departs from the body and stands before the glorious God to be settled in its eternal state. There are twelve hours in the day, as Christ says, during which a man can work, but the night comes when no one can work (John 9:4). The time of this life is your working time, but the night is approaching, and then no one can work. Revelation 6:8 speaks of a pale horse, and the one who sat on it was Death, followed by Hell. Hell immediately follows death for those who are caught in their natural state without having completed the work of making peace with God. 2 Corinthians 5:10 reminds us, "For we must all appear before the judgment seat of Christ, so that each of us may receive what is due for what he has done in the body, whether good or evil." It is not based on what we do afterward but on what we have done in the flesh that determines our eternal destiny. There can be no repentance or belief after this life, as the body and soul are separated, making the whole person incapable of a work of God upon them.

Moreover, immediately after death, God removes all means of salvation. You will never hear another sermon, receive admonition, or have good counsel. There will be no more working of God's Spirit to draw your souls to Christ.

Not only that, but God also withdraws Himself completely in terms of all the common works of His Spirit. This results in a kind of entrenchment of the soul in sin (which, in relation to God, cannot properly be called sin but rather evil). It becomes impossible for you to do anything but sin. Just as the saints, while alive, have many lusts and corruptions within them, yet immediately after death, their souls are so fully possessed by the Spirit that they cannot sin. Conversely, though wicked individuals may have various common gifts of God's Spirit and many restraints while alive, immediately after death, they are so utterly separated from God, and He so completely withdraws from them, that they can do nothing but sin, rebel against God, and blaspheme Him to His face. In Adam's state of innocence, there was a possibility not to have sinned; in our current state while living in this world, it is impossible not to sin. However, in the world to come, the saints have an impossibility of ever sinning, just as the wicked have an impossibility of ever doing anything but sin. Therefore, the wicked must inevitably be situated in an everlasting evil condition. Damned souls in hell cannot do anything but blaspheme God, just as saints in heaven cannot sin against Him.

Furthermore, on the great day, Christ delivers the kingdom to the Father, and there will be a different form of administration than before. Christ will no longer mediate for those for whom He did not mediate in this life. Immediately after the separation of the soul from the body, the Spirit of God completely departs from the soul, and God's wrath is poured out so fully upon it that it breaks the soul and fills every part of it. Due to the overwhelming current of divine wrath carrying the soul along with it, it becomes impossible for the soul to be engaged in anything for all eternity except bearing torment and divine wrath. Just as the saints will be filled with God's presence and carried along by a strong current of divine mercy, making it impossible for their souls to engage in anything other than enjoying God and living for His praise, the opposite is true for the wicked. After death, both are placed in their respective states.

I will not dwell further on the explanation of this point but will proceed to its application, as this point is more applicable than doctrinal. I will content myself with three or four aspects of application and conclude.

First and foremost, we can see the reason we have to thank God for the continuation of our lives, especially those present today who have not yet fully made peace with God and are uncertain about securing their eternal destinies. If there remains any doubt in your heart concerning your eternal condition, and if you have felt the fears of eternity in your spirit, then from the points I have briefly discussed, you will have reason to bless God profoundly, bowing your face to the ground, adoring His abundant grace that you are alive at this moment. Why? Because your life is the time for reconciling with God; it is the time to secure your eternal condition. If your life comes to an end and this work is incomplete, then all is lost, and judgment arrives, leaving you in an irrevocable and ruined state. Therefore, it is truly a blessing that you are alive today. Just as a person with a significant matter to attend to, concerning their entire estate or life, and it must be done in a very short time, would consider it a favour to have their time extended, even if only a little, because their business is of immense importance, and they think to themselves, "If I fail in this, I am lost forever." Likewise, anyone who has ever had serious concerns about the infinite consequences depending on their lives here on earth cannot help but sit down and thank God for extending their lives. For the time of this life is a fortunate time, a day of grace, and a day of salvation. How happy would those individuals, on whom this judgment has already been passed, who are firmly situated in their eternal condition, consider themselves if they could have just one day to make provisions for their eternal estate! They were in your position not long ago, and therefore, know how to value your life. The lives of men and women, especially those who have not yet completed this great work, are worth more than a thousand worlds. I recall hearing about a remark from a great gentleman who was very ill, and when physicians informed him that death was the only way, he said, "Oh, that I might live, even if only as a toad!" Indeed, what man or woman is there who, without having a thorough and scriptural assurance that this great work, making peace with God, has been completed, may, upon being afflicted with sickness, wish to live, even if only as a toad? This is because such significant things hinge upon their lives in this world. Therefore, brethren, just say this to your own hearts when you seriously contemplate what I am currently discussing. What if God were to come now to this congregation and say to each one of you, "Well, the time I have granted you to provide for your eternal estate has come to an end. If you have completed your work, that is good, and you will be saved and inherit eternal glory. However, you will be judged according to what you have done." I fear that if such a message were to come from heaven to many of us, it would cause our hearts to ache, and we would cry out, "O Lord, grant me a little more time before I depart and am seen no more! O that I might have a little more time." Imagine that God had taken you when He took away one of your relatives, neighbours, or friends, and death had arrived, and judgment had been passed at that moment; which way do you think you would have been cast? Can't some of you remember that if God had taken you away at such a time or when someone you knew died, you were in such a condition that you have cause to think you would have been certainly situated in a condition of eternal misery? Therefore, bless God that you are alive today to hear such a doctrine as this one; as long as you live, God gives you time to secure your eternal estate. Psalm 78:38 says,

"But he, being full of compassion, forgave their iniquity, and destroyed them not: yea, many a time turned he his anger away, and did not stir up all his wrath." When sickness befalls men and women, a portion of God's anger is revealed; however, if God had unleashed His anger just a little more, what would have become of you? You would have been lost forever. But God was pleased to withhold His anger, not stirring up all His wrath. Bless God for sparing you at such a time; certainly, if you had died then, your condition would have been as irretrievable as that of the devils themselves. Now is a day of grace, a day when you have the voice of the Gospel and the good news of salvation ringing in your ears. But then you would have been beyond the time of grace, beyond prayer and repentance. Now, as long as you are not beyond this day, you must value your lives. And brethren, understand where the worth of your lives and their continuation lies. Some individuals display terrible impudence, wishing to prolong their lives merely to further satisfy their lusts. Did God grant you life for this purpose? No, the reason you should desire to live is to have more time to make provisions for something of such infinite consequence. If this is not accomplished, it would have been better for you to have been a toad, serpent, or the vilest creature that ever lived. O, if only we had hearts to give God glory for our lives and to appreciate our lives properly, extraordinary results would follow if our hearts were moved in this manner.

Secondly, if the only time we have to prepare for eternity is during this earthly life, then how should those be reproved who waste and squander this precious time on frivolities and neglect the crucial purpose for which they were sent into the world? If such momentous matters hinge on our lives, then the loss of time in our lives is a truly dreadful loss. We all acknowledge that time is precious, and it is indeed so. Understanding and applying this point properly would make us realize just how valuable time truly is. Even if all the pearls in the world were condensed into one, it still wouldn't be as precious as this time of our lives because what depends on it is infinitely more valuable than ten thousand worlds. Yet, despite the significance of time, many people trivialize it, frittering it away in leisure and neglecting their true purpose.

Every moment that you misspend, for all you know, could be the very moment upon which your eternal destiny hinges. When you go out, enjoy yourself, and waste your time, you may be abusing the very moment upon which your eternal fate hangs. If we truly understood this doctrine, we would recognize the great evil and foolishness of misusing our precious time. People often live as if their only purpose in this world is to cater to their physical desires.

Imagine a man coming to a city for a matter of life and death, and the time he has to accomplish it is very limited. How diligently do you think he would spend that time? Each stroke of the clock would weigh heavily on his heart. Now, suppose God were to resurrect a damned soul from hell and give it another chance in the world. God says, "You will live for a quarter, half a year, or even just a month or a week. I will give you an opportunity to make peace with me and escape the misery you're in." How do you think such a soul would spend its time? As you are convinced in your consciences about how such a soul would act, strive to use your time in a similar manner.

Many people seek guidelines to navigate their lives. Consider this rule: if a damned soul could be sent back into the world and have a chance at a different fate, then do what you believe such a soul would do. If someone were to offer him crowns, kingdoms, or even the entire world in exchange for his time, even if it were just a week or a day, he would scoff at such an offer and value one more day above a thousand worlds. Now, you have had days and weeks, one after another, and yet you do not know if you have more than a week or a day left before your eternal fate is sealed upon you. Therefore, there is a pressing need for you to make the most of your time.

How few contemplate the passage of their time or recognize the tremendous significance of the time they have in this world! Consider this: You would deem it utter folly and madness if a person possessed a precious oil worth a thousand pounds a pint and used it to light a lamp for idle talk, play, or frivolous pursuits. Surely, such valuable oil should be reserved for weightier matters. Brethren, the time of your lives is like that lamp, illuminated and sustained by this precious oil. Do not waste it on trifles and vanities. There are matters of infinite importance that you must attend to during your time on earth. This neglect of time is a grave charge against Jezebel in Revelation 2:21, where Christ says, "And I gave her space to repent of her fornication, but she repented not."

I recall the expression of a woman who was in great distress of conscience. When some tried to reassure her that there was hope for her, she gazed at them with a ghastly countenance and said, "Call time again, call time again." It was as if she meant, "If you can call time back, then perhaps there is hope for me." Clearly, we do not fully appreciate the importance of time. An enlightened conscience places great value on time. Nothing can instill a more serious disposition in a person than realizing the worth of their time.

Imagine a group of people sailing at sea, reaching a small island thousands of miles from any other land. They stop to rest on the island, but the mariner warns them not to stray too far, saying, "I will not wait for any of you." The older individuals may be cautious not to wander too far, but the younger ones trust in their swiftness. However, when the mariner departs, they are left behind and perish. Similarly, while we are in this world, we take the opportunity to refresh ourselves. But God says, "Be ready when I call," and God's call is the moment of death. When God calls, some are not ready, and they perish eternally.

The loss of the time of your lives will one day be a dreadful regret. It will pierce your souls to realize that you had a day of grace, but now you have no time left. Judgment has been pronounced, and there is no remedy. There is a story of a woman whose house was on fire. She was busy attending to trivial matters while her child lay in the cradle, forgotten. Later, when she looked at what she had saved, she found a few insignificant things, but then the thought struck her: "What has become of my child?" She feared her child had perished (though it was saved) and was overwhelmed with regret, realizing that she had wasted time on unimportant things and forgotten her child. Beware that this does not become your story. You have been told that time is precious and that there are important matters concerning your souls and eternal condition to attend to. Yet, you spend your time accumulating wealth, seeking pleasure, or pursuing worldly honors. When the final reckoning comes, and God asks, "Now that your time has ended, what have you accomplished in this world?" You may be able to say, "Lord, I have acquired wealth, and I have led a joyous life." But amid all of this, what have you done for your soul? What have you done for eternity? What have you done to make peace with God? What have you done regarding matters of infinite weight and consequence? Your heart will be burdened with the thought that you neglected your soul, spending more time playing than praying to God in private to reconcile with Him. Though you may pass your time merrily here, it will be a dreadful realization in the future when you understand the purpose of your time and why you were born.

Bernard once made a noteworthy statement about people calling to one another, saying, "Let us be merry until an hour has passed." He responded with indignation, "What will you do thus and thus until an hour has passed, until time has passed? Will you squander that which the mercy of your Creator has granted you for repentance, for obtaining grace, and for seeking pardon? Will you waste the time in which you should be striving for the life and blessedness you have lost?" It is fitting for those who have not made peace with God to spend their days lamenting their sinful and miserable condition rather than engaging in revelry and wantonness. How will you wish one day that you had spent your time in mourning and lamentation? As Abraham said to Dives, "Son, remember that thou in thy life time receivedst thy pleasures." This life is not meant solely for sensual pleasures but for reconciling with God. When God graciously grants us time for such significant purposes in this world, He expects all His children to seek His face, make peace with Him, value His mercy, and admire the richness of His grace and goodness in His Son. However, this is not what we observe in most people. It is sheer folly to squander precious time when everything hinges on it.

Thirdly, if after death comes judgment, certainly when death finds any man unprepared in a state of unregeneracy, who has not made his peace with God, it must indeed be exceedingly dreadful because it brings judgment and establishes such an individual in their eternal condition. In Job 18:14, death is referred to as the "King of terrors," and rightfully so, for it is the most terrifying thing in the world to those who grasp the implications of their sinful state and condition. There is enough in this realization to humble even the proudest and most stubborn individual on Earth, as they consider that they are now venturing into the abyss of eternity with little preparation. It may even be the abyss of the infinite wrath of God they are entering, and where they must remain forever. Certainly, except you have a firm assurance of reconciliation between God and your soul, the sight of the infinite abyss you are entering immediately after death cannot help but make you emit a dreadful shriek when you realize that you are now likely to be eternally lost.

When death seizes an ungodly person, it is nothing less than the severing of the thread upon which they hung over the pit of eternal misery. It is the opening of the floodgates of God's eternal wrath. While afflictions may seem like small trickles of God's wrath, death, when it arrives and finds them unprepared, opens the floodgates, and the torrents of Almighty's wrath engulf them. For them, death will be like a sergeant of the Lord of hosts, leading them to prison. It will be like raising the drawbridge, casting them into a dismal and dreadful sunset that ushers

in an eternal night of darkness, with no prospect of dawn. Know that
at death, the day of grace and salvation sets for you, and an eternal
night of dismal blackness and darkness descends upon you. When you
depart this world without making peace with God, you must bid farewell
to all comforts and joys, and everything you once enjoyed. Farewell to
the precious truths of God that were revealed to you, farewell to the
gracious teachings of God's ministers. Farewell to all the dear friends you
cherished, farewell to the times of mercy you experienced. Farewell to
your spouse, children, and loved ones, for you shall never see their faces
again. Farewell to your worldly possessions, house, land, and all delights.
Farewell to the sun, moon, stars, and the entire world. You will never see
them again until you behold them all ablaze on the great and dreadful
day of Christ. At death, the day of grace and salvation sets for you, and
you enter into an eternal night of pitch-black darkness, never to see the
light again.

I am reminded of a statement by Pope Adrian when facing death. He
said, "O my soul, my soul, where are you going? You shall never be merry
again as you once were." It is a mournful thing for a wretched creature,
whose time has run out, not to know where they are going. They think
of past pleasures and delights, knowing they will never experience them
again. When I contemplate the death of an ungodly person, I recall Isaiah
10:3: "And what will you do in the day of visitation?" You may live
luxuriously in the world now, indulging in pleasure and having your way,
scorning the truths of God spoken by His ministers. But what will you
do in the day of visitation when your time in this world comes to an
end? Oh, the change that will come over your spirit! God will regard
you with indignation, saying, "O wretched creature, who spent your days
in vanity, you shall continue in this world no longer. The wrath of the
Almighty is now unleashed upon you." You will be on your sickbed, tor-
mented by an awakened conscience that accuses you of past wickedness
in specific times and places. You will curse yourself for your foolishness

and for neglecting the day of grace and salvation. Your time will be almost gone, and your sickness will intensify. Your friends will gather around, mourning for you. You will grow pale, breathe shallowly, and the devil will await his prey. Your mouth will fall, your soul will depart, and it will be the end of you. An end to all your pride, stubbornness, vanity, and wickedness. This is the fate of those who have not made God their portion. Mercy had its time, but you neglected it, and now you are gone forever.

We often speak of the mercy of God, but is it not a rich mercy for God to grant you, a wretched and sinful creature, such a blessed opportunity for repentance in this world? God called out to you, offering grace, pardon, and peace. He did not extend such an offer to the angels who sinned; when they committed a single sin against God, He cast them away and did not negotiate with them for peace. Therefore, since you have already had your time, let all the angels in heaven, saints, creatures, and even demons acknowledge that God showed mercy to this person, despite the judgment now upon them. O my brethren, the thought of death in this light has much power to affect your hearts. I recall hearing of a person who prayed six times a day. When asked why he spent so much time in prayer, his response was simple: "I must die, I must die." The approaching end of his life, upon which so much depended, was his motivation. O that we had hearts to contemplate this truth, to understand the things concerning our eternal peace even now, in our day, before it is too late. Brethren, these matters are of infinite importance to your immortal souls. May the Lord grant that they have a profound impact on each one of us.

We can apply the dreadfulness of death, which follows from contemplating the point I have been discussing, to various groups of people. Firstly, it should have a significant impact on the hearts of elderly individuals. Your time is near, and you must ensure that your work is completed, for you have little time left to make peace with God. It is like three or four o'clock in your day of grace, and the sun is setting. If a man is about to embark on a journey critical to his life, and he has neglected the morning and much of the afternoon, seeing the sun sinking low, he thinks, "I must hurry now, for if the sun sets before I reach my destination, I am lost, and my life is over." Likewise, those who cross areas where the sea is dry at one time and floods at another, but if they miss by just half an hour, they face death, and when they realize the time is nearly up for the waters to return, their hearts sink, and they say to one another, "We must hurry, for time is almost up." Old men, consider this. You have neglected the time of your youth, and now your time is nearly spent. Take hold of the opportunity while it is still day to understand the things that lead to your peace. Double your diligence now. It is a dreadful sight to see an old wicked man, an old sinner, an old scoffer, an old worldly individual who never comprehended the great purpose for which they came into the world.

Secondly, this applies to all profane individuals who, instead of fulfilling the purpose of their time and preparing for their eternal state, are moving in the opposite direction, widening the gap between God and their souls. If a man must embark on a journey for his life before the sun sets but chooses to go in the opposite direction, he will eventually realize his error and say, "Where am I? If the sun sets before I reach my destination, I am doomed." The same goes for those who persist in profane ways. God has placed you here to live for His glory and to work out your salvation with fear and trembling, but you have gone in the opposite direction, spending your time making yourself even more deserving of His wrath. Take heed, for if you die in your state of profanity, you are lost forever.

Thirdly, this message is for those who once made progress on the path of life and salvation, experiencing a stirring of conscience but, due to the force of their desires, turned back and fell from their previous state. Imagine a man who must cross the sea for his life by a certain time.

Initially, he has a favourable wind, but as he approaches the haven, a great gust of wind pushes him back. How sorrowful is the condition of such a man! Similarly, there was a time when you had a favourable wind. God graciously worked in you through His Spirit, and you seemed to be making progress in the purpose for which you were born. However, the gust of sin and the power of lust pushed you back further than before. Let this awaken you to use your time and opportunities to the fullest for the good of your soul.

Furthermore, this message is relevant to those who, in moments of discontent, wish for death, like some peevish individuals who wish for the grave whenever anything goes wrong. Foolish man or woman, do you realize what you are doing by wishing for the end of your life? You may encounter a different kind of discontentment than what you've experienced here, for after death comes judgment (Amos 5:18). Woe to you if you desire the day of the Lord in a fit of anger, for it may not be a day of light but rather a day of darkness for you. Instead of giving thanks to God for your life, do you wish for death with every sullen mood? This is a great dishonour to the grace and mercy of God extended to you.

Furthermore, this concerns those who, on every occasion of drunkenness or a few heated words, are willing to risk their lives. It is true that fools may endanger their lives for trivial matters because they do not understand their true worth. However, those who comprehend the value of their lives will not do so. I recall a tale about a philosopher who was at sea and faced a life-threatening situation. He was extremely fearful, while the sailors were not afraid at all. They asked him, "Why, are you, a philosopher, afraid when we, uneducated sailors, are not afraid?" He replied, "There is a reason for my fear; if I die, a philosopher is lost. But for you, your lives are not worth much." Thus, those who are willing to risk their lives in a drunken quarrel, yet will risk nothing for God and a righteous cause, do not appreciate the value of their lives, which is why they are so willing to squander them.

Moreover, it pertains to those who, in times of trouble and torment of conscience, are inclined to harm themselves and take their own lives. One would think that this point, when explained and applied as such, should deter such temptations in the future. What an immensely desperate folly it is that someone who is aware of God's wrath and fears it should do something that could lead them irrevocably into it and place them in eternal damnation, as those who take their own lives do. If anyone in the world should desire the preservation of their lives and hold them in high regard, it should be those troubled in conscience. They should pray as David did in Psalm 39:13, "O spare me, that I may recover strength before I go hence and be no more." Use God's own reasoning as found in Psalm 103:13-14, which states that God is merciful to His people because He remembers they are but dust. Therefore, plead with God, saying, "O Lord, spare me, for I am but dust, like the passing wind that shall never return. Now is the time when You have promised to hear. Let my life be extended, for if this time is over, I am gone forever."

Lastly, this concerns those who have believed themselves to be on their deathbeds, facing what they thought was imminent death, and have contemplated this truth. They have seen eternity ahead of them, believed they were in danger of eternal damnation, and felt the judgment in their hearts. However, God has shown great mercy to them and restored their health. Perhaps, when you were in that condition and believed your time was running out, you made promises and said, "Oh, if God would spare my life, I would be a different person! I would use my time differently than before." Well, God has granted you a second chance, and what have you done since? Now, you might be taking God's patience and mercy for granted. Beware, for when your days come to an end, and judgment arrives, it will fall upon you with great severity.

Therefore, my brethren, allow me to address all of you (for I have not come here today merely to spend an hour with you but to benefit your souls). Be aware that this is your day, the day of grace and salvation.

Once again, in the name of God, I declare to you this truth (even if you have heard it many times before): there is not a single person in this congregation, no matter how wicked, who has come before God today through His providence, without the possibility of your sins being pardoned. It is possible for your soul to be saved, for God to be reconciled to you. Today, it is once again proclaimed to you that you are not yet destined for eternal misery, a fate that might have been yours by now. I implore you that when you return home, you would enter your private chambers, kneel before God, and thank Him for this message, once more preached to you.

Beloved, if I or any servant of the Lord were sent by God to the gates of hell with this message, "O damned spirits, know from the Lord that there is a possibility for you to be saved," they would surely listen with joy. However, this message cannot be preached to them, but it can be and is preached to the vilest and wickedest wretch, the enemy of God and goodness in this congregation. God now declares this to you. But how long it will be before judgment comes to determine your fate, you cannot tell. Therefore, know in this day the things that lead to your eternal peace. Who knows what might depend on one day? Prayers and tears may still do you good, but if you delay, even though you cry and howl to God for eternity, it may never suffice. Therefore, recognize the urgency of this moment. It is a fortunate thing for a person to accomplish a task during the right time; among humans, even if a task is completed, if not done in its season, it loses some of its worth and effectiveness. Similarly, prayers, tears, mourning, and pleading for God's mercy lose their efficacy unless they are done in the right time. For all you know, unless you do them today, or tomorrow, or very soon, they may do you no good at all. Therefore, seize this opportunity. God proclaims to each one of you today, "Poor creatures, if you ever expect to receive mercy on the Day of Christ, pay attention now. The golden scepter is extended now. This is the acceptable time, the day of grace and salvation. Come and accept the offers and invitations of grace and mercy now, or you may be lost forever."

Therefore, let this reminder dispel any indifference in your hearts and those wandering tendencies of your spirits that chase after vanities. Just as if a man with wandering thoughts and roving eyes were told, "Sir, consider what you are doing, for it concerns your life; if you go astray, you are a dead man," it would make him collect his thoughts and compose his spirit. Likewise, if you have a light and wandering heart, take this to heart today, my friend, dear soul. Understand what you are doing; even the actions of this day concern your life and your eternal condition. Detach yourself from all worldly concerns until you have completed such a great task. As the Apostle says in 1 Corinthians 7:29-32, "Brethren, the time is short. It remains that both they that have wives be as if they had none; and they that weep as though they wept not; and they that rejoice as though they rejoiced not; and they that buy as though they possessed not; for the time is short." The word used here is that the time is "wrapped up" or "folded up," like cloth tightly folded even to the very end. Therefore, let your hearts be detached from worldly matters. Truly, brethren, those who truly understand themselves would not risk remaining in an unconverted state for even half an hour, even for the wealth of ten thousand worlds. They know that when death comes, judgment also arrives.

And for those of you who are poor, living in hardship and extreme conditions in this world, remember that as long as you live here, your situation is still favorable. You have time to accomplish the work that holds immense significance for the welfare of your souls. Indeed, contemplating this matter should redirect your hearts away from worldly pursuits. It is better for a man to remain here to accomplish that great work, even if it's like a stock or log in the fire, than to be taken away before completing the purpose for which he was sent into the world. When people are in pain, they may desire to die, but if they knew the state and condition of a wicked person immediately after death, they would rather choose to live, even in the most wretched earthly condition.

Furthermore, all you young ones, while God grants you time, should ponder this great task of making peace with Him. If a man were about to embark on a weighty business overseas, after he arrives on the shore, his first thought should be to secure his important task before indulging in merriment. If you have ensured the completion of this great work, that your peace with God is established, and your eternal estate is secure, then you can rejoice among your friends and live joyfully and comfortably all your days. It was once said that art is long, and life is short, but certainly, the art of preparing for eternity is a lengthy and challenging pursuit, while life is short and uncertain. Therefore, do not postpone this great work, as some do. They are always about to take action, they plan and intend, but they never actually do it. I urge you, young ones, to start early. This understanding should drive you to wholeheartedly dedicate yourselves to the great task of your souls. Whatever you do, do it with all your might, as encouraged by the Holy Ghost in Ecclesiastes 9:10: "Whatsoever thy hand findeth to do, do it with thy might; for there is no work, nor device, nor wisdom in the grave whither thou goest." If you ever had a task that required your utmost effort, do it here. Do not just have faint wishes and desires or fleeting good moods, as you might experience when hearing such truths as these. Instead, work out your salvation with fear and trembling, and seize every opportunity, for so much depends on the short span of your lives. Just as it would be utter madness for a man to have a fair day and wind for crossing the sea for his life, yet decide to delay and neglect the wind, thinking he has a few more days to spare, only to find himself without wind when the last day comes. Many think they will repent when they are near death, but beware of neglecting the stirring of God's spirit, for if you do, you may later desire it with all your heart, but it will not return. Therefore, take heed not to neglect this great work. Strive to ensure it thoroughly. For if a man had a task that he could rectify if done poorly, he need not be so meticulous. However, if a man is entrusted with a task that he knows, once it's out of his hands, he can never amend, he will not be careless but strive to make everything certain. Understand that this is true for your eternal condition: what you do in this world must stand for all eternity; you cannot amend it later. If, after realizing your own condemnation, you were to plead with the Lord for more time and a chance to return to the world to correct your faults, God will reply, "No, you cannot return to the world." Therefore, it is of utmost importance to make everything certain while you have the time. Do not rely on blind hopes and reckless ventures, saying, "I hope things will turn out this way or that for me." Instead, entertain the thought, "What if it should turn out otherwise? What if I should fail?" This will greatly humble a person's heart, especially if they know that upon their failure, they are ruined forever.

Furthermore, my brethren, I urge you not to avoid any of God's ways out of fear of suffering. Be willing to endure any hardship for the sake of God's way. How does this follow? Allow me to explain: If the time of your life is the determining factor for your eternal condition, then it is crucial for you to persist in whatever comes your way. For example, imagine a man is on his way to a destination, and he must arrive there by a certain time to save his life. As he rides swiftly through the streets, the dogs bark at him (as dogs often do at those who move quickly). He pays little attention to the barking of the dogs because he is focused on his life-or-death journey. However, if a man is riding merely for leisure, the barking of dogs might trouble him a bit. When a man rides for his life, he won't turn back even if clouds gather and rain falls. He won't turn back if he encounters a dirty and muddy path; he will forge ahead or cross a slough because his life is at stake. But if a man rides solely for recreation and encounters strong winds, dark clouds, and storms, he will turn back. Sadly, it seems that the ways of most Christians in religion are as if they have taken them up for recreation and nothing more. Therefore, when a cloud of trouble and affliction appears, they regret their chosen path and quickly retreat. However, if God were to reveal to you the significance of eternity and what depends on the course of your life here, you would be willing to endure clouds, storms, tempests, and rough paths, all for the sake of your eternal destiny. In conclusion, whenever you are tempted to sin, remember what you have heard today and use it to resist temptation. Say to yourself, "God has shown me today the great purpose and mission for which I entered this world. I understand the immeasurable importance of the things that hinge on the time of my life. Should I then satisfy my own lusts and corruptions, appease the devil and the world, and, in the meantime, neglect that which is of such great importance for the well-being of my soul?" Once again, I wish that you all knew, on this very day, the things that pertain to your eternal peace. Reflect on what has been said, and may the Lord grant you understanding hearts to apply it.

This sermon was preached on April 29, 1641.

FINIS.